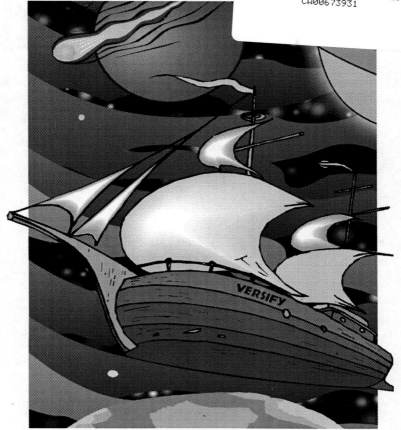

# *POETIC VOYAGES LEEDS*

## Edited by Allison Dowse

First published in Great Britain in 2001 by
*YOUNG WRITERS*
Remus House,
Coltsfoot Drive,
Peterborough, PE2 9JX
Telephone (01733) 890066

HB ISBN 0 75433 256 X
SB ISBN 0 75433 257 8

# *FOREWORD*

Young Writers was established in 1991 with the aim to promote creative writing in children, to make reading and writing poetry fun.

This year once again, proved to be a tremendous success with over 88,000 entries received nationwide.

The Poetic Voyages competition has shown us the high standard of work and effort that children are capable of today. It is a reflection of the teaching skills in schools, the enthusiasm and creativity they have injected into their pupils shines clearly within this anthology.

The task of selecting poems was therefore a difficult one but nevertheless, an enjoyable experience. We hope you are as pleased with the final selection in *Poetic Voyages Leeds* as we are.

# CONTENTS

# The Poems

## DEEP BLUE SEA

Deep blue sea
Crabs nipping nastily
Octopus swimming round and round
Dolphins calling to their friends
With exciting things around
Lighthouses shining brightly
Sharks with their sharp eyes, seeing what's around
Washing waves slushing shores
Fishy smells and sparkling shells
Schools of fish huddling close
In the deep blue sea.

*Rebecca Overend  (8)*
*Armley Primary School*


## THE WEIRD FOREST

Coloured animals, echoes loud,
Soft furnished seaweed leaves,
Roar, banging sounds.
Weird salt leaves,
Rough seaweed banging,
Squid splash in the salty
Seaweed leaves.

*Tammy Gantschuk  (9)*
*Armley Primary School*

## IN THE CARIBBEAN

In the Caribbean,
Hot weather, lots of music,
Jamaican food, lovely time dancing,
Children smell the food,
Dumplin' ackee, rice and peas,
Saltfish, Mum, Dad,
Baby sister and me have a party
And enjoy the time of the Caribbean!

*Candice De Souza  (9)*
*Armley Primary School*

## VIOLENT VOLCANO

Red-hot lava
    Burning fast
Molten rock sizzling, smoking
    Black!
Boulders crashing
    Jungle burnt
All animals dead
    All people fled!

*Jade McCann  (9)*
*Armley Primary School*

## SCHOOL PLAYGROUND

Children playing in the playground,
Playing games like tig, cops and robbers and blocki.
Playing like kittens playing with a ball of string,
Content, happy, like nothing else matters.

Children playing in the playground,
Chattering like parrots about the latest craze.
Talking about school and work,
Talking about new toys and games.

Children playing in the playground,
Pulling pranks behind the Army officer of the playground's back,
Stealthily doing them so as not to be caught,
Laughing like a hyena when it works.

Children playing in the playground,
The bell sounds and faces fall.
In-time has come, the end has come,
Gloomy faces walk into school.

*Michael Evans  (11)*
*Barwick-in-Elmet CE Primary School*


## CRICKET

Fans clapping when they come out to play
Players tossing the coin to decide what they want to do, bat or field
Fast bowling, getting some wickets
Batsmen sending the ball to the boundary
Fielders catching the ball when the batsmen hit it up in the air
Fielders dropping catches and losing games
Batsmen making mistakes and they're getting run-out.

*Matthew Wood  (10)*
*Barwick-in-Elmet CE Primary School*

## FOOD, FOOD, FOOD!

Glorious food
Like chocolate
Ice cream and sweets
I like to eat

Disgusting food
Like sprouts
Carrots and stew
I don't like to eat

Delightful food
Like crisps
And chips too
I like to chew

Repulsive food
Like potatoes
And green beans to chew
I hate them too

Gorgeous food
Like doughnuts
Iced buns and pizza
I like them too

Hideous food
Like vegetables and pie
Onions make me cry
I am not eating them

Chicken nuggets, pizza
Vegetables and pie
Some of these I don't want to eat
But some of these I'll try!

***Stephanie Root  (10)***
***Barwick-in-Elmet CE Primary School***

## Whirling Water

The start of our journey is the start of water in the sea
gushing down to sea like racehorses or a fox after its prey.

First comes the source.
It springs up cool clear water
and trickles down the hillside so softly that anybody
could be sung to sleep by its lullaby.

Next comes the spring.
From a trickling spring to a gleaming clear stream.
It carries on steadily and gently down
the mountainside picking up pace as it goes.

Now we have come to a gorge.
The water has moved on,
now it's eroding earth and rock.

Now the stream has evolved into a river.
Tributaries helping the river on like more racehorses adding to the pack.

We now have rapids bouncing on like a bumpy road.
It's like racehorses pulling down on the track.

Now the water starts to pick up the current.
The waterfall has a beautiful side and a wild side.
It drops like a ton of bricks into the pool below.

One of the most impressive is the meander.
It winds and curves peacefully and gracefully towards the mouth.

Finally we come to the mouth.
After all the time it has taken to come to this point,
the water races into the sea. The race has finished.

*Simon Baxter  (10)*
*Barwick-in-Elmet CE Primary School*

# IN THE PLAYGROUND

In the playground football players are playing vigorously,
taking corners, throw-ins, penalties and free kicks.

Friends running from base to base,
playing tig and using the walls for rests.

Younger children shouting and screaming
like babies at night.

People falling out with friends,
calling them names and meanly making fun of them.

Falling over and tripping over, bruised knees,
grazed hands and a nosebleed.

Soon the whistle blows,
everybody sadly and slowly walks inside.

Football players, shouting children and injured
people go walking into school.

Teacher walking into school
and taking their hats and coats off.

*Laura Sispal  (10)*
*Barwick-in-Elmet CE Primary School*


# LEEDS UNITED

Their team is *Leeds United*
They are extremely cool
They're fifth in the table
And my favourite's *Harry Kewell*

They play at Elland Road
They're faster than the rest
They tackle all defenders
And I think they are the best

I'll have to save my money
And go again because
I really want to see them win
And *United's* Wizard of Oz.

***Christopher Thompson (10)***
***Barwick-in-Elmet CE Primary School***


## WATER

The waves on the sea swiftly flowed.
The sun on the water glowed and glowed.
The rivers ran into the sea in a very bad flood.
The water in the lake was clean and good.
The sharp, speedy stream ran down the hill
Into the lake that was calm and still.

***Sarah Naylor (10)***
***Barwick-in-Elmet CE Primary School***


## ANIMALS

Cows get moved out of fields at 5.00pm on the dot and
the farmers fire up their engines to milk the cows.

Dogs guard houses like lions catching their prey
using their noses to get a scent.

Sheep munch grass all day, making grass tidy.

Cats catch mice scuttling along the floor for their lives.

Rabbits nibble on the mesh of their cages.

Pigs give off a great stench to gas everyone out.

Chickens lay eggs for people to crack and fry.

***Robert Nicholls (11)***
***Barwick-in-Elmet CE Primary School***

## PLANETS

Space is a huge, dark sea, millions of stars
floating and splashing through the galaxy.

Mercury, Venus, Earth.

Hot sun, boiling and bright,
Planets reflecting the glow of this enormous star.

Mars, Jupiter, Saturn.

Photographic spaceships sail to the moon,
investigating the rocky planet.

Uranus, Neptune, Pluto

And the Earth is just a small fish swimming
through the universe.

*Lymara Huckle (10)*
*Barwick-in-Elmet CE Primary School*

## FOOTBALL

Can you guess where I am?
There're frantic fans,
A grubby goalie
Who's very mucky.

There's some superb strikers,
In fact there's one who scored an overhead kick,
It was magnificent.

There's some mighty midfielders,
Some deadly defenders,
All playing on a patchy pitch.

Have you guessed it yet?
Of course you have,
It's a football match.

*Samantha Fozzard  (10)*
*Barwick-in-Elmet CE Primary School*


## THE PLAYGROUND

Strange things happen in the playground,
Bandits rob coaches
And cowboys shoot Indians,
Superman flies around Metropolis,
Sometimes there's a fight,
Time to fly off,
Now someone's in trouble,
Then once I've saved them, I'll leave,
Near the school door,
On some days,
I am the head,
On a great adventure,
To find the lost state,
Round the tall trees,
Through the state's gate.

*Simon Howarth  (10)*
*Barwick-in-Elmet CE Primary School*

## RIVERS

Rivers wide and stately
Muddy and clean rivers
Flowing slowly down
Rippling as the wind blows
The river flows into the sea

Flowing to the sea to be free
Rivers run and run all day and night
Turning and turning, the rivers flow
Slowly the rivers get bigger.

*Candida Ford  (10)*
*Barwick-in-Elmet CE Primary School*


## THE SNOW

The snow is like a big polar bear,
Its fur is like soft snow,
It sparkles like a lovely star,
It's cold and sharp as well,
The icy ponds are him stepping
In the thick snow.

It kicks me,
Punches me and takes my breath away,
Its razor claws scratch me
And its teeth are like jagged icicles.

So just remember, if you feel
The snow's razor claws scratching
At your face, it's the polar bear.

*Antonnia Pelligreeni  (10)*
*Bramley St Peter's CE Primary School*

## THE SNOW

The snow is like a white eiderdown
falling from the sky.
The snow trickles down my face
like an eagle flying.
It is white, bright, glowing stars.
The snow is like a cloud.
It is like a lamb.
It is like a cover, I can wrap myself in it.

*Jade Daniels  (8)*
*Bramley St Peter's CE Primary School*


## THE CHANGES

The weather changes all the time
When it's cold, it's not that fine
The wind it blows all around
The snow starts to fall to the ground
When the sun comes out, it's a lovely day
So I call for my friends to come out and play.

*Jade Fay  (8)*
*Bramley St Peter's CE Primary School*


## FOOTBALL

Football, football, is so ace,
I can play it with my mates,
I play it here, I play it there,
I can play it everywhere.

*Shaun Green  (9)*
*Bramley St Peter's CE Primary School*

## THE WEATHER

The weather is rain,
The weather is thunder,
The weather is cloud,
The weather is snow,
The weather is sleet,
The weather is fog,
The weather is hail,
At last the weather is sun.

*Christopher Nield (9)*
*Bramley St Peter's CE Primary School*


## THE INK IS BLACK

The ink is black,
The page is white,
Together we learn
To read and write,
To read and write.
Every day and night,
That's the way we learn to write,
The ice is lovely and nice.

*Natasha Daniels (10)*
*Bramley St Peter's CE Primary School*


## SNOW

Snowball fight, well I might
Build a snowman, call it Sam,
Got a sledge, slid into the hedge,
Go back to Mum for some hot food in my tum.

Go back outside for a ride,
Don't fall, thanks for the ride Paul,
Now we have to go, we are full of sorrow,
But maybe we can play out tomorrow.

*Amy Metcalf (9)*
*Bramley St Peter's CE Primary School*


# IF

If kisses were water,
I'd send you the sea.
If hugs were leaves,
I'd send you a tree.
If kisses mean love,
I'd send you me.
If love is forever,
Then we're meant to be.

*Daniel Kittsen (10)*
*Bramley St Peter's CE Primary School*


# POOL

When you're at school, you can't play pool
because you're too busy getting told off.
When you're at school, you can't play pool
because you're too busy working.
When you get home, you still can't play pool
unless you've got a pool table.

*Kimberley Lilley (8)*
*Bramley St Peter's CE Primary School*

# THE MAGIC BOX

I will put in my box

The sweet voices of my angelic cousins
The fin of my fish's tail
And the glowing lens from my glasses

I will put in my box

A halo from Heaven's purest angel
The loud laugh of a happy child
The warmest beam from a yellow sun

I will put in my box

The richest gold from Queen Elizabeth's crown
The sparkling silver bell which rang on my auntie's wedding
A bronze medal from the first Olympic games

I will put in my box

The brightest fish ever seen
The first piece of coal ever mined
The black and white stripes of a zebra

My box is fashioned of gold and silver
With jewels and moons on the lid
The hinges are made from shells
In my box I am going to fly around
Through the beautiful white clouds of Heaven
The colour of snow and land on Mars.

*Elizabeth Dell  (9)*
*Bramley St Peter's CE Primary School*

## A LONELY SQUIRREL!

My parents have left me to die,
What shall I say to the passers-by?

Shall I lay and lay
And wait for the long hours of the day.

Or shall I cry and cry,
Until I die.

I haven't got any food,
I'm not in the mood.

To play about,
Seeing my mum I doubt.

When will I see my mum?
There isn't any food for my tum.

Munching on a small acorn,
I wish I had never been born.

What's that munching noise I hear?
It must be getting near and near.

Is that my mum I see?
But how can it be?

As I get closer to the figure,
The figure starts to get bigger and bigger.

As the figure turns around, I realise she's my mum,
So I run up to her and cuddle her tum.

*Faisal Siddiq (11)*
*Bramley St Peter's CE Primary School*

## MY FLUFFY SIAMESE CAT

My fluffy Siamese cat
Can play tennis with a foam bat,
When she misses, she hisses
And when she hits,
I feel down in the pits!

She can also drink out of a cup,
She's as playful as a pup!
My Siamese cat is very soft,
She always sleeps in the loft,
When you tickle her with hay,
She always makes you pay!

My fluffy Siamese cat,
She always deserves a pat,
She's my best friend
And she's never round the bend!

If she's not my best friend,
We'll always mend,
Her name's May
And she likes the bay!

*Fern Pullan  (10)*
*Bramley St Peter's CE Primary School*


## BATS

Bats are black with white fangs,
They live in caves or haunted houses,
They sleep all day and rise at night,
Then they go and give people a fright.

*Shaun Ward  (9)*
*Bramley St Peter's CE Primary School*

## A WILD AND WINDY NIGHT

Rat-a-tat-tat on the windowpane,
came the beat of the wind and the howling rain.

Scared and frightened, I hid under the quilt,
waiting for the rain to stop and the wind to wilt.

Should I? Should I run to Mum,
I'm sure I could make it if I only had the will.

Screeching and howling, bang, bang, bang,
no more courage, I shouted for Mum.

Opening of door, comforting words,
lifted into Mum's arms now, I knew I was safe.

*Abbeygail Pelligreeni (9)*
*Bramley St Peter's CE Primary School*


## IF I COULD FLY

If I could fly, I could see over seas
And tops of tall popular trees.
I could sit on top of the highest mountains
And bathe in some of the deepest fountains.

If I could fly.

I wish I could fly way above the skies
And see the earth below.
I wish I could fly and see with my own eyes
The wonderful sight of paradise.

*Sophie Craven (9)*
*Bramley St Peter's CE Primary School*

## MY FRIEND . . .

My friend thinks she can run fast
and has magic spells that she can cast

That is what I really doubt
that's also what I'm worried about

She even looks like a witch
and always has a terrible itch

My friend has a black cat
and also has a terrible bat

She goes around flying on a broom
that's why I never let her in my room

And also because she might spread a bad smell
she has potions that she can sell

But to me she is a friend
though she sometimes sends me round the bend

At Hallowe'en she might come to scare
so little children please be aware.

*Ayesha Siddiq (10)*
*Bramley St Peter's CE Primary School*


## BOO HOO HOO

Yeah, yeah, yeah, I'm going to the zoo,
Boo hoo hoo, I wish you could come too,
Boo hoo hoo, it's not fair,
Boo hoo hoo, the monkey took my pear,
Boo hoo hoo, it's not fair
Ha ha ha, the hippo's got red and yellow hair.

*Rebecca Edwards (9)*
*Bramley St Peter's CE Primary School*

# THE MAGIC BOX

I will put in my box

The tip of Heaven's whitest cloud,
A beautiful red galloping Egyptian unicorn,
The healthy white glow of a newborn baby.

I will put in my box

The first spark of the first ever crystal,
The last shine of the farthest star,
The floating world with no gravitational ties.

I will put in my box

A sweetie palace with a biscuit garden,
And a sea as green as the grass,
A dazzling blue ice rink.

I will put in my box

A snowman's flower,
The presents from Easter
And the eggs from Christmas.

My box is fashioned from elephants'
Ivory and tigers' stripes,
With stars on the lid,
Dreams and hopes in the corners,
With its hinges made from dinosaurs' skin.

I will dance in my box
With Chinese dragons and Egyptian mummies,
On a planet of my own,
Then end up dreaming in space,
With its purple moon shining in my face.

***Charlotte Walker  (9)***
***Bramley St Peter's CE Primary School***

# BY THE CANAL

By the canal
This is what I see
A dragonfly
Swooping towards me.

By the canal
I hear the sound
Of the birds
Flying around.

In the canal
This is what I see
Fish swimming around
I think they're looking at me.

*Lucy Kay  (9)*
*Bramley St Peter's CE Primary School*


# FISHING

I once went fishing in a lake,
We couldn't catch anything for goodness sake.
We wriggled the bait on the end of the rod,
We prayed all day, please help us God.

We use maggots and squats to bring them near,
But we don't think they're going to appear.
For we haven't seen a thing,
Or heard the bite alarm ring,
Not even a cod, pike or a herring.

It's been a day,
We had to pay,
We haven't seen a thing all day.

*Lee Miller  (8)*
*Bramley St Peter's CE Primary School*

# INDIVIDUALS

Everybody's special,
Millions born a day,
Each of us are special,
In each and every way.

Some think they're too small
And some think they're too slim,
Short people dream of being tall,
Some wish they were stick thin.

Some have long hair,
Others have short,
Some are as good as gold,
While others end up in court.

Some of us complain too much,
Of how we look or feel,
But deep inside we've hearts of gold
And friendships as strong as steel.

*Sophie Lambert (10)*
*Bramley St Peter's CE Primary School*


## FOOTBALL

Football, football, I love to play,
Football, football, night and day,
Even in my sleep, I give it a kick,
Score another goal and I have my hat-trick,
All the fans jump up and cheer,
As me and my mates go for a beer,
Man of the match I was that day
And still the word gets passed around the hay.

*Aaron Parkinson (10)*
*Bramley St Peter's CE Primary School*

# THE MAGIC BOX

I will put in the box

A whisker from a golden cat
The first ray of the yellow shimmering sun
A handful of air that flows everywhere
A colourful cloud that comes from a dream
The first raindrop ever to tip

I will put in the box

The first snowflake ever to fall
And the colourful ray from the rainbow
The first footprint in the snow

I will put in the box

An icicle from an ice cave
The smile of a golden star
A sip from the golden Nile

I will put in the box

The golden glow of the moon
And the silver shine of the stars
A tidal wave from the Pacific
The treasure of a sunken ship

My box will be as tough as steel
As gold as the gold from the rainbow's end
The joints from the first ever dinosaur

I shall fly with my box through the blue night sky
On the birds' road.

*Tom Pullan-Boothroyd (9)*
*Bramley St Peter's CE Primary School*

# I WILL PUT IN THE BOX

I will put in the box

The first raindrop ever to drip
And the first sunbeam ever to be seen,
The end of the rainbow.

I will put in the box

A colourful cloud that comes from a dream
And the bluest part of the sky,
The colours of a newborn butterfly.

I will put in the box

The goldest sun ever seen,
The bluest water ever sipped,
The yellowest flower ever grown.

I will put in the box

The whitest horse,
A frog in a hutch
And a rabbit in a pond.

My box is fashioned of gold and silver,
With pink and orange ribbons around it,
Gold stars on it with diamonds in the stars.

I shall fly in my box
On the whitest cloud,
In the bluest sky,
And land down at Ibiza
And get the brownest tan.

*Leanne Tallant  (9)*
*Bramley St Peter's CE Primary School*

## WAITING AT THE WINDOW

These are my two drops of rain
Waiting on the windowpane
I am waiting here to see
Which the winning one will be
Both of them have different names
One is John and one is James
All the best and all the worst
Comes from which of them is first
James had just begun to ooze
He's the one I want to lose
John is waiting to begin
He's the one I want to win
James is going slowly on
Something sort of sticks to John
John is moving on at last
James is going pretty fast
John is rushing down the pane
James is going slow again
James has met a sort of smear
John is getting very near
Is he going fast enough?
(James has found a piece of fluff)
John has hurried quickly by
(James was talking to a fly)
John is there and John has won!
Look! I told you! He's the sun!

*Emma Stitch  (9)*
*Bramley St Peter's CE Primary School*

## BIRDS IN OUR GARDEN

Robins, sparrows and nuisance magpies,
In wintertime they need some food.

We give the hungry, coloured birds some food,
Of nuts, apples and small pieces of bread.

But where are all the worms?
Fast asleep, down in the deep live the juicy worms.

The worms are unaware of the rain, wind and snow
And the temperature which is low, low, low!

We built a bird table to look after the birds,
To safeguard them from the fast moving cats.

Now we use our binoculars to watch the colourful birds,
Eating our food in the safe environment we have made.

*Deborah Gathercole (9)*
*Bramley St Peter's CE Primary School*


## THE EMPTY SCHOOL

I walk into school and I hear no noise,
I walk up the stairs but there's no pushing and shoving like usual,
I put my coat and bag on my peg but the other pegs are empty,
I go into the toilets and find it is clean,
I go back down to the office but the headmaster is not there,
I go into the other classrooms and find they are bare,
I come back up the stairs and into the cloakroom,
I get my diary out and found it was Saturday today,
Then I walked back home in the rain.

*Nicola Mackey (10)*
*Bramley St Peter's CE Primary School*

## CHOICE

If I could choose what to be,
I would be an inventor,
Then I could use machinery,
Which would make me happy.

If I could choose what to make,
I would make lots of things,
Like new toys and a honey bake,
It would be absolutely great.

If I could choose what to read,
I would read about animals, like bees
And books about growing seeds,
The facts would make me think and think.

The world is full of choices,
It's fun to live in it.
You can hear lots of voices,
Make friends,
Have lots of fun,
This world is great.

*Bethany Clare Nicholson  (10)*
*Harewood CE Primary School*


## CHOICE

If I could choose what I would do,
I would say to Man Utd, 'Boo hoo, boo hoo!'

If I could choose what I would do,
I would play like Rivaldo, the Brazilian Ronaldo.

If I could choose what I would play,
I would play football all day.

*Edward Bramley  (9)*
*Harewood CE Primary School*

## HURT

Today I was hurt,
Both physically and emotionally,
Playing with a friend,
Other friend gets the wrong idea,
I only have a minute to choose,
Should I hit him back? Should I not?
I have nobody to talk to,
I know not what to do,
I feel as though I should run away,
Turn around,
Start again,
But no, I won't,
It'll get better, won't it?
So much choice,
So little time to decide.

*David Ireland  (10)*
*Harewood CE Primary School*


## CHOICE

If I could choose what to do,
I would travel the world with me and you,
I could fly like an eagle and look like a seagull.

I'd visit the Queen
For a cup of tea,
Sitting on her knee,
Till half-past three.

If I could choose
What I could wear,
I'd wear a rose in my hair.

*Katie Mary Beard  (9)*
*Harewood CE Primary School*

## CHOICE

If I could choose where to go,
I'd go to a top high school,
I'd try my hardest day and night
And always do my homework.
I'd listen in my lessons
And always pay attention.

If I could choose what to be,
I'd be a year 6 teacher,
I'd try my hardest to fill their heads
With something that's worth knowing.
I'd get them ready for high school
And they'd pass their SATs by miles.

I have to choose,
Should I choose to be good or bad?
Should I choose to be nice or sad?
Thank you God for letting me choose
And help us choose what is best.

*Abigail Watts  (10)*
*Harewood CE Primary School*


## CHOICES

If I could choose what I could be,
I'd be a cheetah and run with glee.
I'd be a monkey and swing around
And yell real loud and make a bad sound.
I'd be an eagle and storm through the sky
And to all the humans I'd wave, bye bye.
I'd be an ant and scurry around
And creep about and make no sound.

If I could choose what I would do,
When I see Man U, I'd yell 'Boo.'
I'd choose to be a cricketer and score one hundred runs
And then when we have won the match
I'd go home and celebrate by eating cream buns.
You can choose what you can do,
So come on, join in and you choose too.

*Joseph George Watts  (9)*
*Harewood CE Primary School*


## CHOICE

If I could choose where to go,
I'd travel around the world,
I'd stop at France, then at Spain
And end up in America.

In America I'd go to New York
And see the sights of the city.
I'd then travel to Las Vegas
And swim in the turquoise water of a swimming pool.

After that I'd go to Jamaica
And buy a black-coated horse.
I'd travel round getting souvenirs
For friends and family.

I'm now in Australia,
Watching the sun go down,
The gorgeous sands of the beach
Are making me want to come home.

*Emma Hartley  (10)*
*Harewood CE Primary School*

## CHOICES, CHOICES

If I could choose what to be,
I wouldn't please my parents but me,
I'd teach the children from Leeds,
But only because it will make me pleased.

If I could choose what to do,
I'd travel to Canada with only you two.
I'd drop in Niagara Falls,
I'd run into the cafeteria for a dozen spring rolls.

It's great to choose what to be or do,
To be a teacher without the flu,
To do some travelling to Canada without a clue,
You can choose what to do or be,
You can choose along with me.

*Charlotte Melissa Walker (11)*
*Harewood CE Primary School*


## CHOICES

If I could choose what to be I'd be a footballer,
I'd swerve round players,
I'd tackle the players like a bullet.

I'd head the ball,
I'd volley the ball,
I'd run down the pitch like a bullet.

I'd pass the ball, I'd chip the ball,
I'd run for the ball
And I'd run down the pitch like a bullet.

*Matthew Chapman (10)*
*Harewood CE Primary School*

## CHOICE

If I could choose what to do
I would fly like an eagle and look like a seagull.
I would sail to sea
And when I've finished I will go home for my tea.
I will play for Leeds United and be a striker
And then I would meet a hiker.

If I could choose what to do
I would ride a motorbike and go for miles
I would go home and get comfy and watch the X-Files.
Then when I get older
I am going to be as hard as a boulder.
I would go out and get drunk
And I would probably act like a punk.

If I could choose what to do
I would have a look how to make a car
And then I would put down some tar.

*Kieran Jordan  (9)*
*Harewood CE Primary School*


## IF I COULD SEE

If I could choose what to do

I'd see the waves hitting the rocks,
If I could see the dogs and cats playing
I would be very happy
If I could see all the colours of the rainbow
If I could see all the flowers
Like roses, sunflowers, bluebells and tulips
If I could see I would enjoy my life.

*Bradley Treciokas  (11)*
*Harewood CE Primary School*

## CHOICES

If you could choose what you could do,
You could be some cheetahs eating Doritos.
You could be a parrot eating a carrot.
You could be a cat stuck in a hat.
You could be a dog under a log.

If I could choose what I could do,
I would leap and jump and come to you.
I would love to walk and run all day
And be with my furry cat and play.

I like choosing what to do
And you're a human so you can choose too.
Choosing is fun, choosing is good,
But don't choose bad and choose what you should.

*Aruhan Bisengaliev (9)*
*Harewood CE Primary School*


## CHOICES

If I could choose what to do,
I'd be a basketball game and shoot some hoops.
If I could choose what to buy,
I'd buy a pet fly and hopefully it would not die.
If I could choose when to die,
I'd live forever with my fly.
If I could choose how to live,
I'd live in a big house and work hard for it.
If I could choose where to live,
I'd live in Brazil and never sizzle.

*Daniel Nodder (10)*
*Harewood CE Primary School*

## STEAM TRAINS

If I could choose what I would do
I would have a blue new house
I would have a room with trains in it
I'd have a steam train in the back garden

I'd like to go in Mallard's train cab
I'd pay to have it in steam again
It would beat its record
I'd be the driver and make it go fast
I'd make it go slow
I'd stop it in a station
I'd run straight through some stations
It would be fun going faster and faster
That's what I would choose.

*Thomas Gregson (10)*
*Harewood CE Primary School*


## CHOICES

If I could choose what I would do,
I would skip and jump right up to you.
If I could choose what I could be,
I'd be an eagle and fly *whee whee*.

If I could choose what I would be,
I'd be a penguin and swim with glee.
If I could choose what I would do,
I'd be a wizard and magic you.

Choosing is fun, choosing is right,
I'd like to choose from morning 'til night!

*Anna Wilson (9)*
*Harewood CE Primary School*

## CHOICE

If I could choose what to do,
I'd definitely be an excellent footballer,
I'd play for Leeds and score too.
I would choose to be kind,
I would choose to be strong.
I would choose to go on the
Biggest rollercoaster for days and days.
I'd choose to go to sunny, hot America
And stay on the sandy beach.
I'd choose to go in the sparkling sea,
Or I'd choose to make a sandcastle.
I would choose to do a lot of things,
I be you would too!

*Adam Khan (11)*
*Harewood CE Primary School*


## CHOICES

If I could choose what I could do
I would set off round the world on a canoe.

Before I travelled far
I would drive in my car.

Then catch a plane and fly
For miles and miles in the sky.

I would land in Crete
And start to hike.

When eventually I got sore feet,
I would go and buy myself a bike.

*Sophie Chapman (10)*
*Harewood CE Primary School*

## CHOICE

On Christmas Eve they wrapped me up
With some water in a cup,
'Yes,' he screamed I've got a little pup.
He played with me for years on end,
But then I drove him round the bend.

We drove to somewhere late at night,
He threw me out and was out of sight.
What should I do?
I cannot choose.

*Edward Lord  (10)*
*Harewood CE Primary School*


## MY LITTLE CAR

My little car goes far
on the road of tar.

My wheels are round
and go bumpity bump on the ground.

My lights are colourful and bright
and in the dark, give other people a fright.

Once while driving on a country road
I saw a big, fat toad.

I turned to miss him
but instead my car kissed him.

The toad was squashed
so I went home and gave my car a wash.

*Joseph David Dishon  (9)*
*Highfield Primary School*

## FOREST OF SIN

Beware! Beware! The forest of sin,
None come out,
But many go in.

You'll never know what will happen to you,
Even the Splitler
Will be after you.

It breathes out smoke,
Out of its nose.

Other monsters
Will be with him,
So never go in
The forest of sin.

*Ahmed Shehroz Haq (9)*
*Highfield Primary School*


## MY CATS

My cats in our house
Love to catch a mouse,
Fudge is the ginger boss,
Willow likes to play with Floss.
Noodle is the little rascal,
In the night when I'm in bed,
Flossy likes to sleep on my head.
The other cats are asleep in baskets
I love all my cats!

*Ethan Kruk (8)*
*Highfield Primary School*

## AT THE FAIR

I went to the fair, it was scary there,
There were slides that whizzed right up into the air,
Freshening my hair.

Some of the rides banged,
Some went down with a pop
And some zoomed down a vertical drop.

I liked my day at the fair,
Except when my grandad lost his false hair.

Candyfloss everywhere,
Candyfloss in my hair.

Sticky chocolate on my face,
Sticky toffee apples waiting to be eaten.

Swirling, twirling people whizzing around,
Little old grannies on the merry-go-round.

I was sad to go home but there's a lot more adventures to be found,
Can you remember your day at the fairground?

*Emily Walters (10)*
*Highfield Primary School*


## WINTER

W  hite snow lying on the ground
I   cicles hanging all around
N  ights are long and huddled round the fire
T   o see the sun is our heart's desire
E   ventually winter gives way to spring
R   ejoice, let a new season begin!

*Robbie Spowage (7)*
*Highfield Primary School*

## A TRIP THROUGH WILLY WONKA'S CHOCOLATE FACTORY

A trip through Willy Wonka's factory is like
a trip through Heaven!

First I went into a garden full of candyfloss
I saw a chocolate stream and candy canes
But that stream was almost empty because of Augustus Gloop
But little did he know he would get sucked up the drain pipe
Poor Augustus Gloop!

Then we visited a bubblegum room
Over there was another impatient and greedy child
She was called Violet
'Now listen children you're not to eat this gum,' said Mr Wonka
'Well I need to,' said Violet *hand me that gum!'*
As quick as a flash she ate it
She started to blow up like a balloon then she disappeared too.

People don't believe in golden eggs
They think it's a load of nonsense
In this factory it's not
Unlike all the other rooms
This room is full of geese that lay golden eggs
Veruca Salt another ignorant child gets everything in the world
'I want a golden egg and I want it now!'
'Alright Wonka how much for an egg?'
'The eggs are not for sale!' said Mr Wonka
Veruca heard this and let off a riot
She accidentally landed on the egg scale
And passed out as a bad egg
Well Mike Teevee shrunk and disappeared
Charlie Bucket was left, he was a good child
Mr Wonka left Charlie his factory.

*Naimah Qudeer (10)*
*Highfield Primary School*

## LITTLE BABIES

Baby around every corner, screaming in ears so loud
Very cute and cuddly
They make their parents oh so proud
And you better look after them
Because they'll scream over and over again
When they're crying, it's feeding time, so rush because
Time's going by
Why oh why, do they winge a lot?
I think I'd better not ask with all this crying
Stinky nappies everywhere, so I'd better go over there
Now let's go outside,
No Mum, I'm staying inside and I'm trying to hide
Lots of doves look like love for my little baby.

*Emily-Jo Wager  (7)*
*Highfield Primary School*


## MY LIFE

My life is sometimes difficult and sometimes it's easy,
sometimes my homework is easy peasy.

As my brother's wining
the washing machine is spinning.

Matilda is a pain in the neck,
my mum is a nervous wreck.

Mummy is going crazy, reading a book,
She wants some peace and quiet, but I'm afraid she has to cook.

My house is so busy,
we are all crazy!

*Rebecca Oseman  (7)*
*Highfield Primary School*

## THE RAINBOW

When it was a sunny day
With lots of big, fat clouds,
I saw some rain fall from the sky
And colours started to appear.

Out from nowhere
A big arch was filled with colours,
Red as bright as an apple,
Orange as bright as the sun.

Pink as shiny as a rose,
Blue as cold as a snowman,
The rainbow was so colourful,
It made me sparkle inside.

Soon the rain had gone,
As if by magic
All the colours disappeared
One by one!

*Bronte King  (7)*
*Highfield Primary School*


## CATS

A cat is my favourite pet,
At home we have got four.
They like to go out and play
And tease the dog next door.

He often growls and barks like mad,
He claws and scratches grass
And when the cats go and play,
They tiptoe like on glass.

*Matthew Tout  (7)*
*Highfield Primary School*

## WHERE THE BOATS GO

Dark brown is the river,
Golden is the sand.
It flows along forever,
With trees on either hand.
Boats of mine a-boating,
Where will all come home?
On goes the river
And out past the mill,
Away down the valley,
Away down the hill.
Away down the river,
A hundred miles or more,
Other little children,
Shall bring my boat ashore.

*Natasha Jheeta (10)*
*Highfield Primary School*


## FLOWERS

I want a garden of flowers
of many types and colours

I want some to be tall
and some to be small

I want red and pink
and blue ones I think

I will plant the seeds
and pull the weeds
and help to make my garden grow.

*Alyssa Dishon (7)*
*Highfield Primary School*

## GOOD AND BAD CHILDREN

Children, you are very little
And your bones are very brittle,
If you would grow great and stately,
You must try to walk sedately.
You must still be bright and quiet
And content with simple diet;
And remain, though all bewild'ring,
Innocent and honest children.
Happy hearts and happy faces,
Happy play in grassy places -
That was how, in ancient ages,
Children grew to be kings and sages.
But the unkind and the unruly
And the sort who eat unduly,
They must never hope for glory -
Theirs is quite a different story!
Cruel children, crying babies,
All grow up as geese and gabies,
Hated, as their age increases,
By their nephews and their nieces.

*Priya Jheeta  (8)*
*Highfield Primary School*

## WHERE I WILL GO

I will go to a special place,
A place where aliens greet me,
I will fly there in my spaceship,
Stars will shimmer as I fly past
And the midnight sky will look like a desert
As I fly past.

*Sophie Hannah Spencer  (10)*
*Highfield Primary School*

## WHERE ARE WE GOING?

Where are we going to?
I don't know.
Which ever way the wind blows,
That's the way we'll go.

The wind fills the sails,
As we make our way
Across shimmering sea.
Birds and dolphins we can see,
Swimming and jumping and looking at me.

Water splashing as we sail along,
Islands and mountains in the distance,
The sun reflects on the sparkling shore.

I'm anxious now to know,
Where we are going to land.
I really need to know,
Washed up we might be.

Tired and cold are we all,
It can't be far now,
We've sailed a long way.

Heading for the shore,
Dropping the anchor to stay,
So it doesn't get washed away.
I wonder where we are,
The wind has taken us
To forest and sand,
We're all alone . . . I think
It can be ours now,
Our journey's end.

*Andrea Hirst (10)*
*Highfield Primary School*

## TRAVELLING LIGHT

On the coach, sandwiches out,
This will be a busy day, no doubt.
Next the train, on I go,
Come on, faster, don't be slow.
Got to get there, I'm in the fast lane,
Got to catch an aeroplane.
Up in the sky, clouds rolling by,
But no time to look - just fly, fly, fly!
Now I've got a rocky trip,
Across the water, on a ship.
Will I make it? Can I go faster?
I suppose it doesn't really matter.
This is an imaginary journey inside my head,
While I'm sleeping in my bed!

*Danielle Wicks  (10)*
*Highfield Primary School*


## SUMMERTIME

Summertime means sunshine glows
And gentle sand beneath my toes.

Lots of friends come to stay
And come together in joyful play.

Lambs are growing big, strong
Lick lollipops and show my tongue.

Birds singing happily in the trees
How loud is the buzzing of the bees?

All these things say that summer is here
Enjoy them all because God is near.

*Laura Elsworth  (7)*
*Highfield Primary School*

## CHRISTMAS

My mum got me a calendar, so I can count the days go by,
Today it's the 24th and we'll possibly have some pie.
I'm going to bed at 8.00, so in the morning I won't be up late,
I'll leave a carrot and a mince pie out for Santa on a plate.
It's Christmas morning now, I wonder if Santa came in the night,
I look out of the window and oh what a sight.
It's snowing, fluffy white snowflakes down on the ground,
Time for me to creep downstairs without making a sound.
I'm the first one downstairs and I go into the room,
I pick up a present and it feels like a broom.
I see another one with my name on the tag,
It's the scooter I dreamed of with its own special bag.
I've opened all my presents as people start to arrive,
Then after our big dinner, we're going to dance and jive.
The Christmas tree is sparkling for everyone to see,
Now we'll sing some carols around the Christmas tree.

*Katie Elizabeth Higgins  (10)*
*Highfield Primary School*


## TYRANNOSAURUS

I like tyrannosauruses.
They had so sharp teeth they could gobble you up
And they weighed up to 5 tonnes.
The tyrannosaurus was discovered in Mexico,
It lived there around 65 million years ago.
It was the fiercest predator.
His body was very scaly,
His body was 14m long.
He was longer than a house and nearly the biggest thing on Earth.
In dinosaur's time, tyrannosaurus wasn't the largest,
One dinosaur was nearly 10 metres long.

*Liam Duncan  (8)*
*Highfield Primary School*

## UNTITLED

There's a place that I go,
When I'm in bed,
That place is,
Inside my head.

Boats and cars,
An aeroplane,
All of these,
Inside my head.

Voyages on
A pirate ship,
Walking the plank,
Is an ocean dip.

Long and hot,
Desert treks,
Sharp cacti,
Give you pricks.

Lots of thoughts
Around my head,
While I'm in
My comfy bed.

***Pedraam Chamsaz  (10)***
***Highfield Primary School***


## SPORT

I like running and football too
Jumping up and down
Like a kangaroo

Skipping with a rope, skip, skip, skip
Playing a football game
And have a free kick

Tennis is a very good start for the spring
Hitting the ball
With a mighty swing

Sport is very good and keeps you fit
You will be healthy
Strong and really big!

*Simeon Taller (7)*
*Highfield Primary School*


# A Journey In The Sky

Sliding up the colourful rainbows,
Bouncing up the clouds.

Gliding through the air as
Rain begins to fall.

Trees and plants from down below,
Look so small from up above.

Going upwards above the clouds,
The sun is shining brightly.

Going round and round the Earth
Slowly tilting down.

Sliding down the rainbows,
Bouncing down the clouds.

Gliding downwards through the air,
As the rain stops falling.

Trees and plants are getting larger,
Slowing down, fall on the ground
*Bang!*

*Evan King (10)*
*Highfield Primary School*

# A JOURNEY TO INDIA

It was 5.30 in the morning, as we boarded the plane. Excited, as it was my first time that I was travelling by air.

Sat next to window so I could see out.

The engines started, roaring as the plane set for the runway.

The plane started to move, it got faster and faster and faster.

As it took off, I looked out of the window, as the building became smaller and smaller.

Croissants with fresh orange and juice for breakfast, yummy, yummy.

Put on my headphones as I listened to my favourite radio station 'Galaxy'.

Feeling tired, off to sleep without a care in the world.

Lunchtime, as it was my favourite dish, chicken curry, yummy, yummy.

Time to freshen myself, brush my teeth, just like the dentist told me to do so.

Eight hours on the plane, excited that we would be soon arriving in India.

Looked out of the window, no clouds but total darkness.

Excitement filled my heart as the pilot said we were about to land in India.

As I looked out of the window, lights everywhere, buildings getting bigger.

Held on tight to my dad's hand, as we landed in Delhi the capital of India.

My journey from England to India had ended after nine hours.
I didn't feel at all tired, as I was too excited about arriving in India.

*Simran Hunjin (10)*
*Highfield Primary School*


## MY BEDROOM

My bedroom was dirty and wallpaper peeling,
So Mummy said she'd change it and paint the ceiling.
She took down the curtains and lifted the carpet,
But when peeling the paper, wished she'd never started!

My paper before, was also on the door,
But one hundred and one dalmatians, that was the score.
I'm getting taller now, but the dogs were still small,
Did I still want them? No, not at all.

My dogs have all gone now and the walls are all bare,
But we went shopping this weekend and I saw it right there!
It was footballs and players, from top to the bottom,
There was some for Liverpool, but I thought that was rotten!

I decided on England paper, with bedding to match,
This is great stuff, it covers the damp patch.
A football case now, my pyjamas go in
And my new football clock makes such a din.

The clock ticks away and keeps me awake,
I keep waking Mummy who says, 'For goodness sake!'
But not to worry, my dogs have all gone
And they've now changed to footballs that go on and on!

*Ryan McKenna (7)*
*Highfield Primary School*

## THE SNOW

I woke up this morning and everything was white,
the snow came down silently last night.
It covered the road, the grass, the trees,
it covered everything I could see.
I go and get my friends to play
and we run outside in an excited way.
We throw snowballs at each other
and especially at our naughty brother.
We play in the garden and jump about,
we go mad and shout and shout.
We make a big snowman with a carrot for his nose,
we walk around with very cold toes.
We get some pebbles for his eyes
and go indoors for some home-made pies.
We get nice and warm beside the fire,
the snow outside gets higher and higher.
I think I've had enough of play,
I'm staying in for the rest of the day.

*Laura Jade Tindall (9)*
*Highfield Primary School*


## OSCAR AND FIFI

Oscar and Fifi sweet as can be,
It does not hurt when they bite you,
It hurts a little when they scratch you,
They are just so cuddly and cute.

Oscar and Fifi would win in sports day,
They can jump quite high and look quite tall too,
They are actually quite small and their paws are tiny,
They are just so cuddly and cute.

Oscar and Fifi are a bit of a pain sometimes,
They can't stop climbing on the table,
They miaow quite a lot as well,
They are just so cuddly and cute.

*Claire Hutson  (8)*
*Highfield Primary School*


## BILBO'S ADVENTURE

The party starts, seven for tea,
Buns and cakes and cups of tea,
I am confused about this mystery.

The journey begins at the break of day,
Before this adventure starts I've lost my way,
The wizard appears in a flash and says,
'Hurry up or you will be last.'

Deep in the caverns my treasure waits,
Its secrets mine, Golum will hate,
The riddle I asked he could not answer
So the ring is mine from here on after.

The dragon's breath will kill you,
Sting can't help you now, a bare patch on its left breast
Will be the archer's test,
A fierce battle from the air, many people will die there,
The elves and the goblins were beaten well
By the dwarves and the rivermen.

The journey home, the adventure ends,
Back home safe to my hobbit hole at Bagend.

*Josh Hirst  (10)*
*Highfield Primary School*

## HOLIDAY ON THE MOON

We're waiting and waiting
To go to the moon.
Nervous, excited,
We're going very soon.

In the year 2000
It was off to Crete in June.
In 2050
It's holidays on the moon.

We're off now - it's fantastic,
Earth's already far below.
We'll see all the different planets,
Oh look! There's Pluto.

Shooting stars are amazing,
Zooming across the sky.
Going past so quickly,
Whoosh! Another one goes by.

No gravity, we're floating
Outside it's incredible.
Foods floating around,
Different from at home, but still edible.

Stepping on the moon
Is like nowhere I have been.
Are there aliens?
Not that I have seen.

***Rachel Goodhand  (10)***
***Highfield Primary School***

## BABY TALK

When I was two I broked my leggy,
I went to hostible.
My leggy hurt and I doesn't like it,
I doesn't like it at all.

I does like aminals,
I likes elphiants
And hippomopotamuses,
I likes fwimming at the fwimming pool.

It's time for my tummy dinner,
I'm having bobs and neam
And Grandad sausage with digger on,
And lolot for pudding

I talked strangely when I was little!

*Elliot Prior  (7)*
*Highfield Primary School*


## GOOD DEEDS

God loves children
Who care for others,
Who do deeds for goodness
To others

Like lending a hand
To somebody hurt,
Saying kind words
And sharing their pain.

There are many things
We can do for each other
To make life happier.

*Aamir  (7)*
*Highfield Primary School*

## SPORT

When the weekend comes
I love to play sport
I'm really, really good
Even though I'm only short

Football, cricket, rugby too
Oh yes, tennis as well
I cannot wait till Friday
And the ringing of that bell

I love to watch Michael Owen
Then it's into the hall
I have to try and learn
How to swerve the ball

On Saturday it is football
Rugby I think is cool
Oh no, it's Sunday night
And tomorrow it's back to school.
Doh!

*Alex Jones (7)*
*Highfield Primary School*


## BODY

May your hands always be busy,
May your feet always be swift,
May you have a strong foundation
When the winds of changes shift,
May your heart always be joyful,
May your song always be sung,
May you stay forever young.

*Milambo Makani (9)*
*Highfield Primary School*

## GOING SHOPPING

Here we are at the supermarket,
In our car, now let's try to park it.

We are here to do the weekly shopping,
As quick as we can without stopping.

Pushing our trolley around the aisles,
Putting in the food in piles and piles.

We go along the same old route,
Starting with the veg and fruit.

On to fridges of butter and cream,
Lots of yoghurts and margarine.

Behind a counter stands a fishmonger,
Selling cod and haddock and steaks of conger.

Somebody smashes a bottle of pop,
It is cleaned up with a bucket and mop.

Here is a sign,
For some wine.

The frozen food is really cold,
Which makes it difficult to hold.

Tins of meat, bags of pasta,
Near the end, we're going faster.

Walking past the bags of sweets,
Daddy said I could have a treat.

At the checkout, finished our weekly trip,
Now let's go and get some fish and chips.

*Antonia Smith  (7)*
*Highfield Primary School*

## THE SEASONS

The seasons bring such a delight,
Spring, summer, autumn and winter.
I wonder, I wonder, I wonder,
Let's start with winter and let's have a snowball fight!

The glistening trees high above,
Sunsets set in the sky.
Snow that has frosted,
As the sun dies.

The spring has come,
Bright crocuses spread.
The winter is done,
Bright flowers on every flowerbed.

It's summer now, it's nice and sunny,
The flowers grow everywhere.
While bees search for honey,
Now the smell of roses fill the air.

Autumn's here now, here comes the daisies of late September,
Trees have leaves that burn.
Their purples and mauves you will remember,
And reds, browns, oranges and golds at every turn.

In late dull November, flowers are few,
Hedges look so jolly.
So with conifers that strew,
With bright red berries on the holly.

The cycle starts again and again and will remain,
Oh I do hate the spring's rain.

*Alia Sooltan  (9)*
**Highfield Primary School**

## DANCING IN SUMMERTIME

Dancing in summertime is the best
Wiggling and jiggling, singing too
Pointing my toes
Spinning very low
Strike that pose, hold that pose
Oh wow! Those pointed toes
Dancing in summertime is the best
Wiggling and jiggling, singing too
Reaching for the sky
Higher than high
Singing songs to S Club 7
I feel like I am in Heaven
Dancing in summertime is the best
Wiggling and jiggling, singing too
Do it again tomorrow in the warm sun
Dancing in summertime is lots of fun.

*Heaven-Leigh Spence  (7)*
*Highfield Primary School*


## CATS I KNOW

C   ats are nice and furry
A   nd sometimes mess about,
T   hey sit on your lap for a snooze,
S   ometimes they scratch you,

I   like them because they're soft,

K   inder cats don't fight so much,
N   asty cats fight a lot,
O   ften cats purr but some might not,
W   e're the biggest *cat lovers*.

*Laurence Hayes  (7)*
*Highfield Primary School*

## MY BEST FRIEND

My best friend is called Jake
He likes going to the lake
We like to talk
And like to walk.

He likes to run
And have lots of fun
Jake has lots of hair
And needs a lot of care.

He is black and white
And he doesn't often fight
When people knock on the door
He opens it with his paw.

I like to play
And say 'Good boy
Play with this toy.'

*David East  (8)*
*Highfield Primary School*


## IN WINTER

It was a cold winter night,
the sky was white and grey.
The snowflakes danced
as they fell to the ground.
The whistling wind
blew and blew,
till the trees
could not stand still.
The night turns into day,
as the snowflakes go away.

*Autumn Blakey  (7)*
*Highfield Primary School*

## THE SUN

The sun is a golden ball that shines in the sky,
The sun is a flickering light.
It lights up in the day and not in the night,
It shines like a diamond.

The sun is a ball made out of gas,
Without it, there would be no life.
There would be no day or night,
Its rays shine like a bright light.

It rises at first light and sets at dusk,
The sun brings us warmth and heat.

*Nailah Qudeer (9)*
*Highfield Primary School*


## MORNING

I open my eyes to an orange glow,
I get out of bed nice and slow,
I go across the floor
And make my way to the door
    It's morning

Into the bathroom to get myself washed
Teeth and hair all brushed
Down the stairs, bump, bump, bump on my bum
Then my cereal goes in my tum
    It's morning.

*Katie Elizebeth Wildman (9)*
*Highfield Primary School*

# APOLLO 11

On a dark and starry night
The moon shines its rays so bright
As they paused to stand and stare
They wonder what it's like up there.

They thought and planned and planned again
They chose a group of brave, bold men
They built a rocket, power and might
Tried and tested it for the flight.

Motors started, counting down
Held their breath, roaring sound
Moon so large as up they climb
To Earth so small, left behind.

'One small step for man,
One giant leap for mankind'
Those words playing on everyone's mind.

*Kristen Dundon  (10)*
*Highfield Primary School*

# MY CATS

My cats are called Oscar and Fifi,
They've got pads on their paws,
Patterns in their fur
And also they've got sharp claws.

They are both playful,
But not all the time,
They like their food,
But I don't think they'll like lime.

They like different places,
They'll give new ones a try,
Oscar likes it down low,
But Fifi likes it quite high.

*Jamie Hutson  (9)*
*Highfield Primary School*

## ULURU

*(Ayres Rock)*

Uluru is red
As the Aborigines said
An animal sank into the ground
To make the tall, beaming mound
The mountain is a brilliant scarlet pattern
The surface is round and smoother than Saturn.

*Toby Cockill  (9)*
*Highfield Primary School*

## SEASONS

Summer is hot,
Winter is cold,
Autumn is in-between,
But when it's hot and sunny,
Flying all over there're wasps and bees.

Summer is boiling,
Hotter than autumn,
Autumn is cold,
But winter is the coldest season of them all.

*Jessica Crossland  (8)*
*Highfield Primary School*

## ANIMALS

Hippos rolling in water
Monkeys swinging from the trees
Tigers catching each other
Giraffes eating high-up leaves.

Sharks catching their prey
Whales squirting water
Swordfish darting through the sea
Seals feeding their babies.

Dogs chasing their tails
Cats curled up in the heat
Rabbits hopping in the woods
Hedgehogs hiding in the leaves.

Robins flying in the sky
Seagulls swooping over the sea
Magpies stealing shiny things
Blackbirds digging up the worms.

Wake up Dad, have you been dreaming?
Get up and dressed, it's time for work
'Was it a nice dream you were having?'
'Yes, I think so,' was his reply.

*Max Birdsall  (8)*
*Highfield Primary School*


## WILDLIFE

Lions and cheetahs with mighty jaws
Antelope and deer with strongly-built horns
Monkeys and baboons messing around
There is lots of food lying on the ground

Tigers and leopards roaring for food
There will be a lot of food to be chewed
Elephants and rhinos in a stampede
There will be a lot of animals, in lots of need.

*Raza Rafique  (8)*
*Highfield Primary School*


## THE SEASONS

Spring is the time for rain
    showers and newborn animals
In spring there aren't any leaves
    on the ground
Spring is the season when new buds come out
Also Easter is celebrated with chocolate eggs

Summer is the time for warm holidays
    and a hot sun
Some people lie on sunbeds
    to get a suntan
People like it at the seaside

Autumn is the time for falling leaves
In autumn there is Hallowe'en and Bonfire Night
Lots of people go to the park
    to walk and kick leaves

Winter is the time for snow
    and bare trees
Children make snowmen
    and have great fun
Christmas is the time for giving
    and opening presents
The Christmas tree decorates the room
    and we rejoice at the birth of Jesus.

*Natalie Dymoke-Marr  (8)*
*Highfield Primary School*

## CHRISTMAS EVE

C  hristmas is a good time for toys
H  appy and jolly for girls and boys
R  eindeer fly across the sky
I'  d like to see them up so high
S  anta's bringing lots of gifts
T  o all the happy little kids
M  ums and dads hang up the socks
A  s excited kids watch the clocks
S  tephanie wonders how many presents she'll get

E  ven at Christmas she wants a pet
V  elvet fur and big floppy ears
E  xcited we get as Christmas Day nears.

***Stephanie Jade McKenna (9)***
***Highfield Primary School***


## SHARING A PLAYSTATION

Sharing a PlayStation, how hard can it be?
It's always your turn, but when will it be me?
You play for ages and I always lose.
What game shall we play?
You always choose.
We argue about it every day
And you always want your own way.
Mum says, 'Stop it or put it away!
That is enough for today.'
I don't like sharing a PlayStation with my brother,
Next Christmas, Santa *please* bring me another!

***Sophie Wicks (7)***
***Highfield Primary School***

## MY BROTHER!

My brother's very naughty
He drives me up the wall,
Of all the brothers in the world
He's the worst one of them all.

My brother's football mad,
He wants to play for Man U!
He practises very hard though,
I think he'll make it, do you?

My brother's love is chocolate,
He would eat it all the time,
My mum's got a different opinion,
She'd rather eat a lime.

I don't always like my brother,
Although sometimes he is okay,
But when he drives me round the bend
I send him out to play.

*Hannah Elizabeth Jones (9)*
*Highfield Primary School*


## A WORLD OF SNOW

Tiny snowflakes pouring down,
Spinning, twirling round and round.
Frozen lakes, thick and cold,
Houses with heaters all been sold,
A light, white blanket gently forms,
Parents try to keep in the warmth,
Broken sledges going slow,
I wish I could live in a world of snow.

*Jane Ann Almond (9)*
*Highfield Primary School*

# FOOD

I like breakfast
I like tea
I like putting
Food in me.

I like cornflakes
I like toast
But I like my egg
The most.

Slice the top off
Poke about
Pull the dripping
Yolk right out.

I like breakfast
I like tea
I love putting
Food in me.

*George-Thomas Guilherme-Fryer (9)*
*Highfield Primary School*


# JESSIE

I have a pet cat,
Who always has food,
She plays on the mat
And never gets in a mood.

She sleeps on my bed
And plays with my things,
She purrs if she's not fed
And I feed her the food she brings.

She plays with my shoe
And is always ready to eat,
She plays with my teddy because it's blue
And tries to bite my feet.

*Moya Hannah Speak  (8)*
*Highfield Primary School*


## INDIA'S QUAKE

From boom to doom
in forty seconds.
From smiles to sorrow
in forty seconds.

From the world of hustle and bustle
to stillness on the ground
in forty seconds.

From high-rise flats
to heaps of concrete slabs
in forty seconds.

From happy families
to orphans
in forty seconds.

From laughter of happiness
to cries of pain
in forty seconds.

This is the land that the Earth
dealt to the people of Gujarat
in forty seconds.

*Aarti Sonigra  (9)*
*Highfield Primary School*

## UP ABOVE

Up above and round about,
You can hear the space call shout.
It makes you want to go up there,
Where aliens live without air.

Up above and round about,
The golden sunrays shine throughout,
Sparkling on pearly balls,
Also on mountains and on halls.

The planets whirl and dance around,
Making not a single sound.
Round about and up above,
An atmosphere which sings of love.

Huge rockets fly high until late,
Shimmering diamonds lie in wait.
Up above and round about
And then the moon comes slowly out.

*Helen Elizabeth Gregory (9)*
*Highfield Primary School*


## VOYAGE LIMERICK

There was a yellow sailor
Who had a wife called Leila
He went around the world
And had his hair curled
That curly, yellow sailor.

*Robert Hirst (10)*
*Highfield Primary School*

## FRIENDS

I have all sorts of friends,
big, small and tall.
Every one of them is nice,
and they rule.

Friends are very important,
otherwise you'd be sad
'cause you'd only have your mam and dad.

Every day you play with your friends,
but if you don't, you just sit alone,
wishing you had a phone.

*Abigail Melcher (8)*
*Highfield Primary School*


## SNOW

There was a weird light,
I got up out of bed,
Why was it so white?
I opened the blinds,
It was so bright,
When I looked, I shouted, 'Hooray!'
It was snow.
I am going to have so much fun,
I am going to snowball fight
Or make snowmen or go sledging,
'Oh no' I have school today.

*Geoffrey Ewan Belcher (10)*
*Highfield Primary School*

## WAVE GOODBYE TO WINTER, SAY HELLO TO SPRING

Winter has gone
The beautiful sunset that blazed in the sky
And the winter is done.
Flowerbeds growing up to the sky,
I see birds dancing in the air,
I can see bees scratching their knees,
Flowers are growing everywhere,
I love t he start of the new season.

*Ismail Sooltan (7)*
*Highfield Primary School*


## ARTY THE ALLIGATOR

A   rtychoke is my name
L   udo is my favourite game
L   emons are my favourite fruit
I    look like a very big boot
G   oing underwater to catch fish
A   s fish and chips are a tasty dish
T   he shore is where I go to sleep
O   ctopus always come and peep
R   ivers are such a great place!

*Sam Llewellyn (7)*
*Highfield Primary School*


## AN APPLE PIE

My nana made an apple pie,
It wasn't wet, it wasn't dry.
She made it in a little dish,
Right next to a plate of fish.

There were no apples to be seen,
It smelt just like a pile of bream.
She realised what she had done,
She started laughing with lots of fun.

*Melanie Elizabeth Coen  (9)*
*Highfield Primary School*


## SIOBHAN

S    iobhan is a young girl
I    think she is quite funny
O    h what is she doing now?
B    ut now she's all alone
H    ow she understands I really do not know
A    nd she's always very lively
N    ow she's very quiet.

*Clare Ockendon  (8)*
*Highfield Primary School*


## A POEM ABOUT ME

One day I went to the park,
and I went on a swing,
then I went on a climbing fame and
went on a twirly wheel.
I went home and was sick
for the whole week.
My mum brought me loads
of magazines and sweets
and I went to my grandma's
and slept there.

*Emily Crabtree  (8)*
*Highfield Primary School*

# No, No, No To Smoking
*(In memory of Grandpa Arthur)*

Say no, no, no to smoking
But why should you do that?
Because smoking cigarettes makes your blood sticky
Because smoking cigarettes can stop you walking
But why should they do that?
Because smoking cigarettes can give a disease to your legs
Because smoking cigarettes makes your heart work harder
Because smoking cigarettes can make you have a heart attack
Because cigarettes have tar in and it's dangerous for your lungs
Because smoking cigarettes can give you lung cancer
Because cigarettes have nicotine in, which is a drug
Because smoking cigarettes makes your hair smell
Because smoking cigarettes makes your clothes smell
Because smoking cigarettes makes your fingers yellow
Because smoking cigarettes makes your house walls go yellow
Because smoking cigarettes is very expensive
So what could you buy instead of 20 cigarettes every day?
You could buy a Dreamcast console each month
You could buy a PlayStation 2 in 10 weeks
You could buy a mini scooter in 2 weeks
You could just save £30 a week
You could buy loads of sweets but they rot your teeth
So what do you think?
Is it good or bad to smoke?
I say no, no, no to smoking.

*Andrew Hobson  (9)*
*Highfield Primary School*

# PET POEM

I have a cat called Sam,
He likes to eat lots of ham.
His fur is soft and sleek,
His nature mild and meek.

When playing on my violin,
He dances like a shark's fin.
When blowing down my flute,
He sits and glares in my boot.

I have a dog called Jack,
He likes to be tickled on his back,
His fur is rough and spiky,
His favourite toy is a bear called Mikey.

When walking in the park,
He runs wild and lets out a bark.
When he is muddy I make him take a bath,
He splashes around and makes me laugh.

I have three goldfish in a bowl,
Flipper, Supersonic and one called Sole.
They swim around all day and night,
But can be seen better in their light.

They have big bulging eyes and wispy fan tails,
When I feed them fish flakes they surface without fail.
Blub, blub, blub, their mouths open wide,
Gobble up the fish food, head up with pride.

*Zoe Starkie  (8)*
*Lawns Park Primary School*

## BEARS

Polar bears
Honey bears
Jungle bears
They're everywhere

Shy bears
Crying bears
Brave bears
And even bare bears

White bears
Red bears
Blue bears
And even running
through the woods
a green
bear.

*Rebecca Hill  (10)*
*Lawns Park Primary School*


## BUG LOVER

All the things I love about bugs!
Bug finder, bug binder, bug minder.

All the things I love about bugs!
Ant eater, worm eater, mayfly eater.

All the things I love about bugs!
Bug dasher, bug basher, bug masher.

*Matthew Shaw  (11)*
*Lawns Park Primary School*

## ALARM CLOCK

A   rgghh! Time to wake up!
L   azy brother it is 7am
A   m I awake?
R   eady to go to school
M   orning Mum.

C   ook my own breakfast
L   ate for school shouts Mum
O   ur teacher does the register
C   hooses Cheree to take the register
K   eep quiet children.

*Muniba Farrukh  (7)*
*Lawns Park Primary School*


## MY CAT

My cat is like my very best friend
that will always stay by me.
When I'm sad, he's always bad
but that's OK for me.
Sometimes he's boring,
sometimes he's fun!
That's when he makes me happy,
that's really fun for me!
He's the best friend for me.

He'll always be the very
best friend for me.

*Rachel Evans  (9)*
*Lawns Park Primary School*

# MY DOG

My dog is the best dog of all
All the time he barks and yelps he just wants his ball
My dog just loves to munch on bones
When he barks, he barks in tones
He's a cheeky pest, but he is the best
My dog is the best dog of all.

*Samuel J Feeney (11)*
*Lawns Park Primary School*


# THE TREE OUTSIDE

The tree outside is round and fat
and taller than the others.
It's outside our house facing the road.
It's blue and spiky,
taller than me or you.
It's beautiful I can say,
it stands there just to sway.

*Heather Bright (7)*
*Lawns Park Primary School*


# FIREWORK POEM

Fireworks, fireworks, sparkling bright
Up, up and away, up in the dark night
Look at the stars sparkling bright
Bang, bang, bang, with a crash in the night
Red, blue, yellow and diamond white
All these beautiful colours amidst all the fright.

*Jade Linley (9)*
*Lawns Park Primary School*

## ANIMAL ALPHABET

A is for ape that climbs up ropes,
B is for bear that rolls down slopes
C is for cat that knelt down and bowed,
D is for dog that barks very loud,
E is for elephant whose trunk is so long,
F is for fox that is very strong,
G is for giraffe that has a long neck,
H is for hummingbird that has a hard peck,
I is for iguana that has a long tail,
J is for jay that likes to eat snails,
K is for kookaburra that sits in a tree,
L is for lion that won't chase me,
M is for monkey that messes around,
N is for newt that is hard to be found,
O is for ostrich that goes to sneak,
P is for penguin that has a smooth beak,
Q is for quail that has feathers on top,
R is for rabbit that goes hop, hop, hop,
S is for salmon, they swim in the river,
T is for turtle, like a snail they slither,
U is for unicorn, it has a big horn,
V is for vole that is newly born,
W is for whale that has a water spout,
X is for X-ray fish that looks inside out,
Y is for yak out in all weather,
Z is for zoo where they all live together.

*Jamie Bright (10)*
*Lawns Park Primary School*

## WHAT IS THE WEATHER TODAY?

What is the weather today? Sunny, rainy or windy;
What is the weather today? Wet, cold or dry,
The fluffy clouds are so low I can see them float by!

Can you see the birds fly?
Can you see them flutter by?
They only come out when it is sunny,
When they squeak they sound so funny!

As soon as there is thunder,
The animals go under;
Dig down deep
And go to sleep!

*Matthew Cousins  (9)*
*Lawns Park Primary School*


## PLANETS

The sun is bright, golden and light
The moon has a silvery glow
Where it goes in the day, I don't know

Mars is a dusty red planet
Where nobody lives on it
Looking in the sky I can see stars
I wonder which one could be Mars

Planets, Pluto, Saturn, Mercury
Others too
But it's Earth that we live on
That is me and you.

*Kelsey Thackray  (7)*
*Lawns Park Primary School*

## ROCKET POWER

Shooting up high as fast as light,
The rocket flies into the night.

Everyone was full of joy,
Every little girl and boy.

Off they flew up to the moon,
They would be there very soon.

When they got there, what would they see?
It was all a mystery.

When they got there, what would they find?
This was an adventure of the very best kind.

*Michaela McKue  (11)*
*Lawns Park Primary School*


## FROM THE SKY

Slow as a tortoise in the sky,
Watching farms and fields pass by.
People walking through the grass,
Cows eating as they pass.
Dotted sheep with their lambs,
Piles of wood like beavers' dams.
Children playing as good as gold,
On the grass that looks like mould.
Helicopter landed from the sky,
Finally safe from way up high.

*Jade McNichol  (10)*
*Lawns Park Primary School*

## MY SISTER

My sister is someone who I
play with when I'm bored
and keeps me company
when I'm abroad.
Sometimes she's annoying
sometimes she's funny
and sometimes she gives
me the funniest looks.
She messes up my bestest
books and sometimes if
she's so bad, when I'm mad
I just ignore her. Ha! Ha!

*Amy Pullan (9)*
*Lawns Park Primary School*


## FLOAT ON WATER

A boat as slow as people walking,
From a far distance you can hear
people talking.
While you're floating on the sea,
you can see loads of trees.
In the forest you can see animals
proud, happy and free.
In the sea you can stay day and night
and start to steer when it becomes light.

*Clare Louise Williams (10)*
*Lawns Park Primary School*

## BONFIRE NIGHT

Fireworks, fireworks all around,
Up above and on the ground.

Rockets zooming all over the place,
Trying to count each one . . .
As if in a race.

Spirals spinning to and fro,
Watching them . . . go, go, go.

Sparklers lit up all around,
Some in hands and some on the ground.

Watch the fire roaring,
Way up into the air,
The flames light up the sky tonight
And the fireworks they glare.

Toffee apples and parkin,
Pies and mushy peas,
Yum, yum, yum,
We all love these.

Dangers lurk around the corner,
The night is still so young,
The fireside is hot and bright,
But we're all having fun.

Not everyone is happy now,
The fire's burning out,
Watch out . . . watch out . . . watch out . . .
*Danger's still about.*

***Charlotte Benn (10)***
***Lawns Park Primary School***

## THE CORMORANT

The sea was blue,
When I looked at you.
You were standing on a rock,
Just out of the dock.
You were standing very still,
With a slightly hooked bill.
At first I thought you were dead,
But then I saw you shake your head.
You spread your wings then dive so fast,
How long underwater could you last?
You are dark black,
But unlike a duck you don't quack.
When you came up from beneath the sea,
You turned around and looked at me.
Now your feathers are wet and sleek,
You've caught a big fish in your beak.

*Elliot Dawson  (10)*
*Leeds Grammar School*


## THE OTTER

The otter,
Sleek and silent,
It dives,
Up and down with merely a splash,
It lands in the water,
Using a rudder like a tail,
To guide it,
The lutra snaps up a fish
And glides back through the water,
Sending ripples as it goes to the Lutra Holt.

*Alex Peel  (10)*
*Leeds Grammar School*

## THE MODEL CORMORANT

The cormorant is standing ready to dive,
Sitting in the children's hands,
Standing alone on a rock,
The children stand there wondering
While the bird never moves, not an inch!
The bird man, the strange man . . . the bird man?
All he needs is the wood,
Give him the wood and he's off!
Carving at top speed he creates
Many birds all on perches.
Some come, come all,
Come on, come see,
Some brilliant craftsmanship with me!

*Cyrus Kay  (10)*
*Leeds Grammar School*


## MY FRIENDS ARE PLAYING IN THE SUN

My friends are playing in the sun.
My friends are playing in the sun.
Hooray, hooray, hooray.
My friends are playing in the sun.
My friends are very silly now.
My friends are very silly now
Because Billy made them silly now.
I don't know why
And I don't know how.
Billy is playing very silly
With my friend, Milly.
He's a silly Billy!

*Ashleigh White  (8)*
*Miles Hill Primary School*

## MY DOG

My dog can bite,
My dog can bark,
My dog can fight,
My dog can roar.

My dog's the cleanest,
My dog's the bestest,
My dog's restless,
My dog's lively!

My dog's a terrier,
My dog's a staff,
My dog's a house pet,
My dog protects.

*Niela Hussain  (8)*
*Miles Hill Primary School*


## PARROTS IN TENERIFE

Amusing parrots in Tenerife,
Colourful birds in Tenerife,
Parrots perform shows,
Audience clap and clap.

Parrots prepare tricks in Tenerife,
Hot blue sky, the parrots fly,
Colourful feathers flapping high.

The colourful parrots dance and dance,
They fly and fly,
They'll make you smile,
By and by.

*Natalie Reed  (9)*
*Miles Hill Primary School*

## THE FLASH OF LIGHTNING

One night two girls went to bed
And then a flash of lightning said,
'I'm coming down to scare you there!
I'll crash, I'll flash, I'll bang!
I'll see you here,
I'll see you there.
I'll come and crash,
I'll crash in the moonlight,
I'll crash in the sunlight,
I'll crash in the night,
I'll crash in the evening,
I'll crash at noon,
I'll crash all day long.
I'll crash here,
I'll crash there,
I'll crash anywhere.
*Crash! Crash! Crash! Crash!*
That's what I'll do!
Ha, ha, ha.'

*Zoe Welsh (8)*
*Miles Hill Primary School*


## GHOST TOWN

There was a horrible town
With no people in it,
The buildings were tumbling down,
It sounds like a ghost town.
We should leave now,
We will bump into each other,
We should get a torch.

*Milly Felton-Glenn (8)*
*Miles Hill Primary School*

# PARROTS IN TENERIFE

Parrots in Tenerife,
Parrots in Tenerife,
They can fly so high,
They flutter and soar
In the light blue sky,
They're funny, colourful and they squawk.

Funny, funny birds, show your tricks,
Wow, wow, children smile.

We enjoy the birds when they make us laugh,
We love to see them fly so high,
Birds, birds everywhere.

*Alex Woods  (9)*
*Miles Hill Primary School*


# THE HAUNTED HOUSE

In the scary haunted house
there was a little field mouse,
creeping along the dark wooden floor
to the squeaking creaking door.
The poor mouse had a dreadful fright
from the bright blue light,
which looked like the sky.
The shock made the poor wee mouse die!
Poor, poor mouse!
You should never have gone
To that scary haunted house!

*Bobbie Elmslie  (9)*
*Miles Hill Primary School*

## TERRAPIN AND HIS FRIENDS

Terrapin, Terrapin,
Where are you?
I'm still asleep in my rock pool,
A tiny starfish tried to warn,
Terrapin still asleep dreaming of stars,
The tiny starfish saw a little red crab,
The starfish thought of a little nip
To wake the terrapin up,
The tiny starfish rolled to the crab
And told the little red crab about Terrapin,
The crab gave Terrapin a little nip,
Terrapin woke up with a little snip,
Octopus came out from the sea
And bought them all an ice cream each.

*Jennifer Wright (8)*
*Miles Hill Primary School*


## GOOD RUGBY

Rugby players are fast.
Rugby players are fat.
Rugby players get hurt.
Rugby players score.
Rugby players get points.
I was a star for my team
And then I scored a goal
And celebrated and won
And cheered because we won the match.
We won the match.
We won the match, we won, we won, we won the match!

*Ross Hammill (7)*
*Miles Hill Primary School*

## SCHOOL

School is fun in different ways,
We even have our very own trays.
We have sharpeners to sharpen our crayons,
Red, black, yellow and blue.

I like maths, DT and swimming too,
They all help to teach you.
I like the way the teachers are nice,
They always have kind smiles.

*Keeley Hill (9)*
*Miles Hill Primary School*


## THE WINTER TREE

The old tree in winter
Stands higher that the other trees.
Its crinkled leaves are small insects,
Its trunk as fat
As an elephant's body.

The branches point
To the heavens above.
The rough rotting bark
Makes the tree seem older
Than it actually is.

The old tree in winter
Is looking too old.
It becomes dimly aware
Of the chop of the axe;
Soon the tree will be gone.

*Niall Oddy (11)*
*St Francis RC Primary School*

# FEEL THE WORLD

Feel the tinglyness of a velvet coat
Feel the point of a Viking boat
Feel the smoothness of a wooden table
Feel the stickiness of a sticky label
Feel the hardness of a steel bolt
Feel the crystals of a pinch of salt
Feel the fur of a wild boar
Feel the blade of a metal saw
Feel the breath of a panting wolf
Feel the soldiers of the Gulf
Feel the power of Hitler, the loser
Feel the breath of an old boozer.

*Dan Irwin  (10)*
*St Francis RC Primary School*


# THE WONDERFUL TREE

The wonderful tree
As the winter begins
I start to get colder
And I start getting worried
Because all the children are going inside
They're not playing outside with me
I used to love them swinging on me
And climbing up, but now they have disappeared.

*Amber Davey  (9)*
*St Francis RC Primary School*

## THE FOX'S WISHES

I wish my life would be kinder,
Then my dreams would all come true,
I'm not as nasty as people make me out to be,
I can't help being sly,
It's a natural instinct.

I disagree with fox hunting,
I'm constantly in fear,
I'd get caught, sliced and diced for fun,
I wouldn't mind as much,
If they hunted me down for food.

They are building roads everywhere,
I'm scared of being hit by a car,
Almost every day I see my brothers and sisters
Laying down on the road injured,
Most often dead.

I see a car coming at me,
I hear the tyres of the car
Screeching against the road
When the brakes get slammed on,
But it is too late, it hits me.

*Dominic Kioseff (10)*
*St Francis RC Primary School*


## WINTER OAK

An enormous skeleton swaying in the howling wind.
Great gnarled branches reaching to grab you.
Bare witch-like fingers pointing to the sky.
Blowing violently until spring begins.

*Alex Bussey (9)*
*St Francis RC Primary School*

## THE OAK TREE

The oak tree is happy
In the summer sun,
Watching all the children
Having lots of fun.

Now the autumn's coming,
It's getting a bit colder,
He's just a bit unhappy
Because he's getting older.

Oh no, here comes winter,
It's freezing cold out there,
Poor, unhappy oak tree,
He thinks this is unfair.

Look, now spring is coming,
His leaves are growing back,
He's happy now the winter's gone
And summer is on its track.

*Kelly Mulligan (9)*
*St Francis RC Primary School*


## THE WINTER TREE

The tree sways from side to side
With all its hair falling out
Upon a blanket of just pure white.

The wind blows once again
With a coating of icing
Covering its arms which are
Drooping down in a sorrowful way.

*Emma Atkinson (11)*
*St Francis RC Primary School*

## THE SQUIRREL'S DREAMS

I run as fast as I can just to get away from my fear,
I have no family nor friends,
They got lost in this twisting world,
With those eyes in the darkness,
In the darkness staring all around,
I'll probably do the things they did and get lost,
You think I'm a free creature,
But you've got me wrong,
I'm the total opposite,
I'm trapped,
Caged with fear
And please do me a favour,
Help me,
Don't be those eyes.

*Tom Cliff (11)*
*St Francis RC Primary School*


## THE TREE

The tree is swaying from side to side,
Watching over the grass.
The tree's arms are drooping,
The tree looks miserable,
The cold wind swerving through the branches,
The leaves are going with it.
A rainbow appears with the sun,
The tree shines with pride,
The tree's arms come up and the tree stands straight.

*Jessica Adcock (10)*
*St Francis RC Primary School*

## CAGED

I sit in my cage thinking about what it would be like to live in the wild,
To run free and to explore,
I am a little fat and not so fit
As I don't get much exercise
And lots of sleep
To taste the juicy grass on the green
And the excellent feeling of freedom.

*Katie Sparkes (11)*
*St Francis RC Primary School*


## THERE WAS AN OLD MAN FROM SKYE

There was an old man from Skye,
Who wanted to learn how to fly.
But when he got in the plane,
He gave a great cry of shame,
'Cause he hadn't kissed his mother goodbye.

The old man then went back into his house,
Where he sat down on a large tailless mouse,
Then he had a fantastic dream,
That he was building a flying machine,
But too scared he then ran out of the house.

The old man decided to follow his dream,
To build this fantastic flying machine,
But he didn't get far,
So he borrowed a car,
And went fishing for cod in the stream!

*Calum Arthur Langan (7)*
*St Oswald's CE Junior School*

## WITCHING HOUR

I woke up suddenly from my sleep,
I heard a noise go squeak, squeak,
Then I heard another noise,
It was coming from beneath my toys.
I put the cover over my head,
Then something bony touched my bed.
It pulled and pulled and pulled at me,
Then it grabbed me by the knee.
I really struggled to get free,
And then I saw a ghostly face staring right at me.
I tried to make a loud scream,
But I was frozen like ice cream -
I looked at my clock shaped like a flower,
It was midnight, witching hour.

*Stella Fozzand  (8)*
*St Oswald's CE Junior School*

## THINGS THAT GO BUMP

Under my blankets
Deep in the night
I hear a bump
I shiver with fright
I see the clouds pass over the moon
I hope to go to sleep soon.

*Natasha Martin  (9)*
*St Oswald's CE Junior School*

## MY HORRID COLD DAY

Freezing fingers,
Frost on the ground.
Icebergs in the ocean,
Snow all around.

Winter's here,
Wrap up snug.
There might be snow,
Are you sure you're warm as a rug?

Icicles in the distance,
Snow out of sight.
Footprints on the ground,
Hail! Hail! Wrap up tight.

*Nikita Colley  (9)*
*St Oswald's CE Junior School*

## VAMPIRES

Very still in the dead of night
A vampire lurks between the moonlight
Monstrous bats with long pale faces
Big, red, horrible teethmark traces
Parents worried about the children's skin
That's what happens in those nights within.

*Kayleigh Dempsey  (7)*
*St Oswald's CE Junior School*

## SLEDGE RIDE

Up with the snow
Down with the sun
Christmas has gone
Winter's just begun!

And I'm out . . .
Sledging faster with my friend
Over the hills and drifts around a bend!
Fall off, roll over with my buddy
Oh no, we've landed in something muddy!

Up with the snow
Down with the sun
I'm really tired
Now winter's begun!

*Judith Tattersall (8)*
*St Oswald's CE Junior School*

## LIGHT AND WATER

Light like fire, water like rain, fire burns,
Water puts it out.
Sphere like the Earth, cone like a party hat,
Circle like a screw top, square like a cross with no outline.
Cube like a dice, rectangle like A4 plain paper.
Old scruffy curtains like old rags,
Snakes like wiggly lines.

*Ben Gilboy (8)*
*St Oswald's CE Junior School*

## WELCOME TO EGYPT

Welcome to Egypt
Let's open the door
And look at the pyramids
I've got in store.

There are also the tombs
With pictures in stone
And the pharaohs of Egypt won't
Leave them alone.

There's also the river
Called the River Nile
That helps all the people
And makes them smile.

Inside all the houses
There isn't TV
Or sloping roofs
Or electricity.

When people die
They are put in a case
In the shape of a man
With a happy face.

The weather in Egypt
Was mostly hot
'And did it rain?'
No, it did not.

*Charlotte Wright  (8)*
*St Oswald's CE Junior School*

## KIM'S PONY

Kim had a pony,
its skin was white as snow.
She rode it every morning
and fed it every night.
They galloped through the fields
and trotted down the road.
Kim loved her pony very much.

*Jessica Watkinson  (7)*
*St Oswald's CE Junior School*


## THE SEA

Enormous-swallower,
Stafish-curler,
Fish-bubbler,
Wave-swirler,
Shark-muncher,
Eel-electrifer,
Swordfish-fighter,
Sea horse-driver,
Squid-squiggler,
Ferocious-whale killer,
Crab-scuttler,
Turtle-surfer,
Dolphin-diver,
Sea slug-squealcher,
Shell-keeper,
Coral-climber.

*Harina Zoey Panesar  (11)*
*St Paul's CE Primary School*

## THE SNAIL

Steady-walker
None-talker
Gentle-groover
Smooth-mover
Shell-hider
Slow-rider
Slinky-sneaker
Slow-creeper
Slipstream-maker
Gardener-hater
Long-sleeper
Secret-keeper
Silent-stalker
Moonlight-walker.

*Lauren Turner  (11)*
*St Paul's CE Primary School*


## MY BIG SISTER

My big sister, big and brave
Wears white shirts and mini-skirts
She wears lipstick red as blood
And big earrings as big as hoods!

She wears blue nail varnish as blue as the sea
And she always invites her friends for tea

My big sister is the best
She is the best sister because she's *mine!*

*Danica Cooper  (10)*
*St Paul's CE Primary School*

# DOG

Attention-seeker
Nosy-peeker

Face-licker
Flea-picker

Fur-heater
Greedy-eater

Tree-marker
Loud-barker

Tail-wagger
Teeth-dagger

Muddy-walker
Cat-stalker

Water-gulper
Great-sulker.

*Nicola Clarkson  (11)*
*St Paul's CE Primary School*


# LITTLE MISS FAILURE

Little Miss Failure
Flew a plane to Australia
And crashed it right into the sea
'Phew' she said with sweat on her head
'I'm so glad there's no passengers with me!'

*Melanie Myers  (11)*
*St Paul's CE Primary School*

## GUESS THE ANIMAL

Little-sniffer,
Burrow-digger,
Fur-grower,
Ball-roller,
Grass-hopper,
Carrot-muncher,
Nose-twitcher,
Water-drinker,
Baby producing is a habit,
Have you guessed?
Yes, it's a rabbit.

*Grace-Ann Bryan (11)*
*St Paul's CE Primary School*


## FLOPPY

Floppy our rabbit
Has a very funny habit
She tips up her food
When she is in a bad mood.

*Rebecca Ellis (10)*
*St Paul's CE Primary School*


## PARODY OF HUMPTY DUMPTY

Humpty Dumpty sat on a wall,
Watching West Ham United,
Paulo di Canio put one away,
Humpty was delighted.

*Alan Garratt (11)*
*St Paul's CE Primary School*

## PARENTS

Make-up-keeper
Snoring-sleeper
Lovely-cooker
Baby-lover
Money-loader
Warm-cuddler
Gentle-speaker
Polite-eater
Job-hater
Great-stresser
Brill-thinker
Tea-drinker
Loud-shouter
Bad-doubter
Homework-helper
Story-teller
Good-dancer
Rubbish-prancer
Clothes-worrier
Newspaper-gossiper
Kettle-watcher
Fun-spoiler.

*Abigail Naledi Rinomhota  (11)*
*St Paul's CE Primary School*

## MY PONY, DAVID

I am very lonely when I'm not with my beautiful pony.
He always greets me with a neigh and his colours are a lovely grey.
A longer mane you've never seen, it floats in the wind like
a wonderful dream.
His tail flies behind him like a swishing sail and his nose is as
pink as a pretty rose.
While I'm busy with my study, my pony's getting very muddy.
We have to work in a team to get him sparkling clean,
Then I put on his saddle and in the winter puddles we go for a paddle.
At the shows, he is very giddy, he's on his toes with his pretty bows.
He always catches the judges' eye, they always say 'Isn't he lovely!'
with a great big sigh.
Then with our rosettes we go home and before he goes to bed,
he has a comb.
Before he's fed I'll have to make his bed.
Before I go home I kiss him and when I get home I miss him.

*Jade Lauren Brierley (9)*
*Sharp Lane Primary School*


## SKY AT NIGHT

Sky, sky, sky at night,
Stars shining very bright.
The moon glows softly in the sky,
Shining brightly ever so high.

The biggest star appears in the north,
It's the first to shine so very bright.
Other stars will come out tonight,
Sky, sky, sky at night.

*Gemma Beanland (10)*
*Sharp Lane Primary School*

## My Dad

I know this man, he's called my dad,
He really isn't all that bad.
He drives around in his big, white van,
He is a very jolly man.
He's not very good around the home,
Except for talking on the phone.
He calls us boys his double troubles
And his favourite place is a bath full of bubbles.
In summertime he lays in the sun
And likes to watch us having fun.
He really is an awful pest,
But to me he is the best.

*Jonathan Brine  (9)*
*Sharp Lane Primary School*

## In The World

In the world we're all different,
Everyone's different you see.
I'm not the same as he or she
- There's only one of me.
Even if you are twins
You only look the same,
But inside you are special,
Unique in your own way.

*Danya Wilson  (10)*
*Sharp Lane Primary School*

## A MESSAGE TO THE PEOPLE OF THE WORLD

The world is disappearing every single day,
Surely the people of the world don't want it that way.

The car fumes making asthma worse,
The mobiles cooking brains,
Children being brought up with a curse
Of different acid rains.

Animals are disappearing from the land and sea,
What will there be left in the future for children like me?
The rainforests of the world are quickly depleting,
Children are starving to death,
While we are over-eating,
Children are so cold you can see their breath,
We just turn up the heating,
We're melting the ice-caps of the planet,
Put all of us people in a pot together, we'd made a giant gannet,
*So please take care or there will be nothing there to share!*

**Charlotte Robbins  (10)**
**Sharp Lane Primary School**


## THE STORM

I am the lightning, crumbling and crackling beneath your feet.
I send forks of lightning down, making pictures in the sky.
I am the lightning, watching people run inside.
Look at me, I'm the king of the sky.
Hear the lightning crumbling, crashing and thumping down to Earth.
I am the lightning, fierce and evil.
Feel yourselves trembling from head to toe.

*Josh Harper  (9)*
*South Milford Primary School*

# THE STORM WOLF

The wind was a wolf,
Howling his eerie song into the night,
As he raced across the darkening sky.

The sea wolf threw himself against the shore,
Time and time again,
As the sea wolf reared up then came crashing down,
Into the waves.

The storm wolf's snarl echoed through the night,
As thunder and luminous lightning
Flashed in his menacing eyes.

Torrential rain came pounding down,
As the sea wolf reared up then came plunging down
Right over the high harbour wall,
To devour the village.

*Beth Waters (11)*
*South Milford Primary School*


# BLIZZARD

I am the blizzard, fierce and evil,
Big grey clouds and swirling snow.
I am the blizzard, twisted and evil,
Heavy rain, lots of hailstones.
Hear me whistling as I send the wind.

I am the blizzard, cold and bold,
Everything I touch turns to ice.
I am the blizzard, king of the sky,
Watching people run inside with fearsome eyes,
Seeing the storm that I am brewing.

*Keir Bills (10)*
*South Milford Primary School*

## THE ISLAND EATER

Thrashing waves
Claw at our island,
Dark storm clouds
Bring a downpour,
Freezing water
Crashing down on us.

Blustery gales
Swirl around
Like a sandstorm,
Thunder booms,
Lightning bolts,
Our electricity flashing.

Hailstones pound
On our faces,
Blizzards tumble
Over us like a blanket,
Bursting banks
Flood dangerously
Over our beloved island.

Stubborn winds
Go back and forth,
Thunder and lightning
Die down,
Naughty winds
Flee from sight,
As the sun
Comes through,
After having
Won his battle.

*Catherine Hardy  (10)*
*South Milford Primary School*

## SEA STORM

I am the storm on the sea
That's who I be
I can send horrible gloomy rain
To send you to your doom in pain.

I send flashes of lightning
Which are terribly frightening
Plus booming bolts
That come zooming down.

When I calm down from being angry
I end with a little frown
Then I disappear like I haven't ever been here.

*Emma Towers  (11)*
*South Milford Primary School*

## THE SNOWSTORM

The polar lands come alive
with a raging snowstorm.
Swirling over timeless forests
and unclimbed mountains.
As white as the whitest snow.
As cold as the coldest ice.
Covering everything in its path,
like a suffocating blanket;
turning water into chilling ice.

*James Pawson  (10)*
*South Milford Primary School*

## THE STORM DRAGON

I am the storm dragon,
  My mouth bursts open and
    Hailstones bounce out,
  I send thunder when I am angry.
I am the storm dragon,
    I send torrential rain when I breathe
  And I send snow blizzards with my tail.
I am the storm dragon,
    I send great floods when I cry,
    I drench everyone wherever I go,
  My claws send hailstorms when they
      touch a cloud.

When the storm is finally over I go
  to *sleep!*

*Natalie Idle  (11)*
*South Milford Primary School*

## THE STORM TIGER

The storm tiger lets the black clouds out
The angry tiger drenches all
The hungry tiger lets out the rumbling of thunder
The eyes of the tiger are like the flashes of lightning
The powerful tiger sent hailstones in his anger
The mad tiger never stopped, he sent great floods
The strong tiger sent blizzards of snow
Then all of this stopped, the angry storm tiger was asleep.

*Becki Tierney  (11)*
*South Milford Primary School*

## THE STORM

I am the threatening storm cat,
I roar like the strong king of the jungle,
I burst over-flowing riverbanks,
I grip and rip young trees' branches.

I am cross, angry and dark,
I switch the bright, flashing lights on,
I drop my bouncing hailstone marbles,
I send blizzards which are closing curtains to eyes.

I leave the spraying hosepipe on,
I sob and weep torrential rain,
I drown houses under deep water,
I am the storm dragon of the sea.

*Emma Jones  (10)*
*South Milford Primary School*

## THE ROYAL STORM

I am the king of storms,
I bring the rain and thunder,
The rain pounces down, like very heavy snow,
The thunder roars like vicious lions waiting for their prey.

I am the queen of snowy days,
I make you *very* cold,
The blizzards are like autumn leaves
Falling on your head.

*Charlotte Hannah McGarrity  (10)*
*South Milford Primary School*

## THE STORM WOLF

Rain came down, it was like
the storm wolf's feet crashing
to the ground with a sudden *bang!*

Lightning flashed as if the storm wolf's
powerful eyes were flashing as they watched you.

The wind whistled as the storm wolf began to roar.

The sea crashed against the rocks,
as the storm wolf began to scratch.

Then the storm wolf drifted away in the night.

*Laura Louise Collins  (11)*
*South Milford Primary School*


## THE STORM

I am the sleet and the snow,
I will give you my worst wrath.
My thunder will strike you like a 1000 volts,
My hail will hit the ground like meteorites.
My powerful wind will whistle like a loud flute,
I am angry, my winds will get bigger,
My hail will get faster and the thunder will get louder.

*I will get you,*
*I will get you.*

*Harry Roe  (10)*
*South Milford Primary School*

# THE SNOWSTORM

The high howl of the wind was
as noisy as a pack of wolves.
The storm was a tiger waiting
to pounce.
The sky was filled with angry
black storm clouds.
The snow flurried against the
window with a sound like fingers
brushing the windowpane.
Cold, feather flakes lay on the
ground like a huge white blanket.

*Matthew Liddle  (11)*
*South Milford Primary School*

# THE STORM DRAGON

I am the storm dragon of the sea,
I plunge houses into deep water,
I devour small fishing boats when I'm hungry,
My eyes flash brightly and split trees.

I am the storm dragon of the sea,
My dangerous waves drown tiny people,
My thrashing tail causes chaos in towns,
When I roar I sound like an angry lion.

*Amy Phillips  (10)*
*South Milford Primary School*

# I'M AFRAID OF . . .

I'm afraid of
  savage dogs with big sharp teeth.

I'm afraid of
  the darkness under my bed where creatures lurk.

I'm afraid of
  falling off a cliff onto the jagged rocks below.

I'm afraid of
  squeaking mice that shuffle along the floor at night.

We're afraid of
  reading this out in assembly.

*James Rich  (9)*
*South View Junior School*


# THE FOUR SEASONS

Spring is the time when baby lambs are born,
Spring is the time when flowers grow,
Spring is the time when the leaves grow on the trees.

Summer is the time when kids play outside,
Summer is the time when people are going on holiday,
Summer is the time when kids have water fights.

Autumn is the time when the leaves fall off the trees,
Autumn is the time when it is harvest,
Autumn is the time when it is Hallowe'en and Bonfire Night.

Winter is the time when it is Christmas!

*Thomas Large & Jack Hutchison  (9)*
*South View Junior School*

## CLASSROOM

Teacher - yelling
Children - chatting
Rulers - snapping
Pencils - dropping
Pens - writing
Draws - pulling
Heads - thinking
Books - opening
Clock - ticking
Playtime - coming
*Bell - ringing.*

*Donna Cope  (10)*
*South View Junior School*

## THE TIGER

In the deep dark jungle
Lives a fast and fierce beast,
Crash! Boom! Bang!

He runs like the wind
And roars as loud as thunder,
Crash! Boom! Bang!

His stripes the shade of burning fire,
Eyes as mean as devils,
Crash! Boom! Bang!

*Esta Owen  (9)*
*South View Junior School*

# WRITING A CONTRAST POEM

Out in the corridor
where nothing moves

like a deserted desert
and the floorboards creak

like a cat's miaow
a spider spins a web

casting a spooky shadow

and it gets longer
and longer

here in the classroom
where all hell has broken loose

like a football match when someone scores
and the noise gets louder

like a siren closing up on you
a teacher screams

making a high-pitched noise

it gets louder and louder.

*Jake Alvin  (10)*
*South View Junior School*


# THE SUN

Shining brightly in my eye
A yellow ball in the sky
Above the clouds, way up high
The blazing sun passes by.

*Thomas Spence  (8)*
*South View Junior School*

## LOUD AND QUIET

Out in the countryside
where the sheep all graze
like fluffy clouds in the sky
and the horses run
like a person trying to win a race
a sheep grazes
and baas
and baas.

Here in the city
where the people all shout
like a crying loud baby
and the feet all move quickly
like a marching army
a person falls to the ground
with the crowd
with the crowd.

*Aime Brook  (11)*
*South View Junior School*

## PENGUINS

Penguins swim,
Penguins glide,
Penguins toboggan,
Penguins slide,
But most of all penguins . . .
Sleep all day,
Just like you!

*Emily Chappel  (8)*
*South View Junior School*

## MY POEM ABOUT THE SUN

The sun is bright, red and fierce,
It's in your eyes, on your head but not in your ears,
Sometimes we just don't know what to do
Until the sun comes out and shines on you,
Then we play and have lots of fun,
Until the sun goes in and then we're done.

*Rebecca Houston  (8)*
*South View Junior School*


## WINTER

W   et, cold days
I    ce, frozen snow
N   ights come so quickly
T    rees are so bare
E    verything you see glittering and sparkling white
R    eal snow is *brill!*

*Lauren Jones  (8)*
*South View Junior School*


## SOUND

Television blaring out in the room
baby crying downstairs
people fighting with each other
people shouting outside
dogs barking, running up and down the garden
I can hear through the walls
children yelling loudly next door.

*Lee Edwards  (11)*
*South View Junior School*

## QUIET AND LOUD

Out at a disco
Where music bangs
Like the Second World War
And lights flicker
Like searchlights scouring the city
A balloon drops
And it falls
And falls
*Bang!*

Out at the pub
Where nobody goes
Like a sweet-smelling countryside
And you can hear the sound of a mouse scuttling
Like the quiet footsteps of children sneaking downstairs
A child trips
And falls
Falls.

*Rebecca Drake & Joanna Mason (11)*
*South View Junior School*


## DOWN TOWN

Here in the city,
where cars shoot past,
like rumbling volcanoes
or an athlete running his best,
like a dog running for its life,
or a spaceship heading for space,
a car crashes
and a person dies.

*Ryan Deighton (11) & James Whitehouse (10)*
*South View Junior School*

## THE HAUNTED HOUSE

In the lonely corner of the haunted house
where all is silent
like an abandoned cemetery.
Bat wings flutter
like cobwebs in the breeze,
and the frozen ghost lurks!
Waits
and waits!

Outside the wind howls triumphantly,
hitting the boarded windows
like a steel ball!
The rain tapping on the roof
like loud gunfire!
Louder
and louder!

*Darren Hargett (10) & Nicholas Garside (11)*
*South View Junior School*

## TEACHERS

How come teachers always drink tea,
Or maybe even coffee?
In the staffroom chatting away
And then when the bell rings they always say,
'In that staffroom I've been working through play.'
But I never believe them,
I just say they've been drinking cups of tea,
Maybe even coffee.

*Alishia Schofield (8)*
*South View Junior School*

## THE DISCO

Out in the alleyway
where a ghastly shadow sits
like a tiger awaiting to strike its prey
and the mouse scurries towards the bin
like hungry men at their dinner
eating and eating.

Here in the disco the music blasts out
like an air raid siren
the girls dance to the music
like wolves howling to the moon
a light is shining up to the ceiling
flashing and flashing.

*Jade Kershaw  (11)*
*South View Junior School*


## NATURE IS NATURAL

Some shells are big, some are small,
Some are flat, some are tall.

Some sands are dark, some are light,
Some are dull, some are bright.

Some waters are white, some are blue,
Your reflection looks like you.

Some animals are small, some are big,
Some animals swing from twig to twig.

*Gillian Brook  (9)*
*South View Junior School*

## A Cat, A Mouse, A Dog

Running through
the field,
the cat is being
chased by a mouse,
the dog is being
chased by a cat,
very strange potion
they drank, it all
turned around
from dog chasing
cat, cat chasing
mouse, to mouse
chasing cat, cat
chasing dog.
This is very strange
indeed, all you
need is another
potion and *bang*
the cat, the mouse
and the dog, mouse
and dog will be
back to normal but
just one thing I
forgot to tell you
don't feed it or
give it water OK.

*Sarah-Lee Bailey & Kerry Michelle Wood  (9)*
*South View Junior School*

## I Am Afraid Of . . .

I am afraid of shadows that seem to dance around the room.
I am afraid of Dracula with teeth as sharp as razorblades.
I am afraid of wind and rain lashing against the windows
like ghosts tapping on the door.
I am afraid of poltergeists throwing things around the room.
I am afraid of my bed creaking all night like
people moaning and groaning.

*Louise Baines  (8)*
*South View Junior School*


## Anger

Anger is as black as the night sky on a cold night in November,
Anger smells like gone-off potatoes two years out of date,
Anger tastes like dandelion juice in your mouth,
Anger is someone on the drums never stopping,
Anger feels like lots of pins sticking in your face,
Anger lives in the centre of the Earth shouting and throwing
                                        lava everywhere.

*James Grimshaw  (11)*
*South View Junior School*


## Untitled

The moon sparkles in the sky and gives twinkles in your eyes
It looks like a great big light, the one that I switched on at night
The moon is everywhere I go, watching me I know
When I come home late at night, it shows me the way to go.

*Sam Driver ( 7)*
*Summerfield Primary School*

## SEASONS

In winter you
splash in puddles,
it is very
icy and cool.

In spring it's getting
warmer, the flowers
start to bloom.

In summer it is
hot and you can
play with all your
mates.

In autumn the
leaves fall off
the trees, the
ground is in
a state.

*Amie Victoria Parkin (9)*
*Summerfield Primary School*


## PLAIN JANE

I am just a little girl
Who lives on the lane.
People often stare at me,
Maybe because I'm plain.
It really doesn't matter,
When I hear them chatter.
Although my name is Stephanie,
They think my name is Jane.

*Stephanie McHale (9)*
*Summerfield Primary School*

## MY CAT, COOKIE

Fluffy and ginger with little white paws
Its main weapons are its little claws
On the sideboards, on the desk
You wouldn't know such a pest
It's not caught a rat
It's not caught a mouse
But it's caught the love in this very house.

*Thomas Owen  (9)*
*Summerfield Primary School*


## MY DOG

My dog is called Spice
It is very, very nice
It likes licking feet
That are very, very sweet
It likes squeaky toys
That are not for boys.

*Charlotte Fowler  (8)*
*Summerfield Primary School*


## WHY?

Why do kids go to school?
Why do dogs sit and drool?
Why does the sun shine so bright?
Why do we have day and night?

Why do balloons float so high?
Why do birds fly in the sky?
Why do cats chase mice?
Why is ice cream so nice?

Why do cats and dogs get fleas?
Why do we have to say thank you and please?
Why do babies sit and cry?
Why do people have to die?

*Samantha McHale  (10)*
*Summerfield Primary School*


## THE NEW GIRL

I am the new girl at Summerfield School.
Everyone thinks the deputy head is really cool.
Mr Farley is his name.
I think he would do alright on the Generation Game.

My teacher is called Miss Bright.
At first she gave me a terrible fright.
But I soon settled down
And got rid of my frown.
I wish I could say the same about Mr Brown.

Every Monday we go swimming at Bramley Baths.
It makes a change from doing maths.
Cross stitching is not my thing,
But oh boy can I sing!
One day I made an Indian pot
And now I'm learning about cold and hot.

The headteacher is called Mrs Barley
She is a bit like Jacob Marley.
Work, work, work, that's all we do.
No time to rest you've got to do another test.

They say my handwriting is too small.
I'll just have to buy a bigger pencil, that's all!

*Hannah Barran  (8)*
*Summerfield Primary School*

# MR MAY

I have a teacher called Mr May,
He always tells us what to play,
So when we're stuck, we would say,

'What do you say Mr May?'

When we're working and it's hard,
The answer's usually on a card!
So when we're stuck, we would say,

'What do you say Mr May?'

When we've come out with the flu
And we ask Mr May what to do,
When we're stuck, we would say,

'What do you say Mr May?'

When it's playtime and we're bored,
We have found a piece of cord,
'I'm sure we could use this in some way,

What do you say Mr May?'

We do PE, it's really fab!
But I can't quite yet do the crab.
So when we're stuck, we would say,

'What do you say Mr May?'

When we're cooking, we look in a book,
I can take over from Mum (she's such a bad cook)
But when we're stuck, we would say,

'What do you say Mr May?'

When we've all finished our lunch
And we ask Mr May for a bit of a hunch,
'Make your own mind up for just one day,
How about you go and play!'

*Ella Watkins  (11)*
*Summerfield Primary School*


## RUFUS

Rufus is a dog
Who hasn't any friends.
He howls all day,
From beginning to end.

He has no one to feed him,
He's all skin and bone.
He just wants a new friend,
He doesn't like it alone.

He lives in a dump,
Which isn't very fair.
He just howls and howls,
'Does anyone know he's there?'

He hasn't any friends,
He's all skin and bone,
He lives in a dump,
He just wants a new home.

*Richard Gartland  (9)*
*Summerfield Primary School*

## SNOW

Snow, snow, when will it come?
In the wintertime I said to my son
It comes in storms or during the night
And when you awake the ground is
Covered like a Christmas cake
I hope it snows on Christmas Day
Then Santa can ride his sleigh
He will bring us presents
And lots of fun
But most of all he will say hello
And a ho, ho, ho
Then back to Lapland, back to the snow
That's where he will go.

*Matthew Rodley (8)*
*Summerfield Primary School*


## HOMEWORK

I had a sheet of homework
but couldn't get it right,
I stared and stared and stared at it
uncomfortable all night.
I read it once, I read it twice, I read
it till it hurt my eyes,
I couldn't find the answers no matter
how I tried.
My mum said it was time for bed
I looked at her and shook my head,
'Climb inside and rest your head
there's always tomorrow to do it instead.'

*Andrew Fields (10)*
*Summerfield Primary School*

## MY LITTLE SISTER

M ind of a monster
Y ou could say she's the minx of the world

L ook at her beautiful big blue eyes
I mpossible to say no to
T akes no notice of what you say
T ells you what to do
L ives by her own rules
E very day she has the same cheeky face

S mells sweeter than sugar
I rresistable in every way
S uch a cutie
T empts you to do anything
E verything she does is the funniest
R uffled hair whenever you see her.

That's my little sister!

*Alex Lavelle  (10)*
*Summerfield Primary School*


## UNTITLED

Birds are flying
All around
Some are heading southward
Bound
Some will die
Some will not
Some will arrive where
The weather's hot.

*Christopher John Fletcher  (8)*
*Summerfield Primary School*

## MY DREAM

I had a dream and this is it,
there was a witch,
her name was Titch.
Titch had a long nose,
even longer than her toes.
She had a broomstick,
it was called Loonitick.
She had a finger,
who thought it was a singer.
She had a black cat,
just like a black boat.
She had a bat, who was called Tat,
he lived in a hat.
Just then I woke up in the middle of the night
and had a . . . *fright!*

*Lauren Godfrey  (7)*
*Summerfield Primary School*


## JASPER THE DOG

I've got a dog called Jasper
Who likes lots of pasta
Jasper likes lots of tea
And he is three
Jasper is black, he chases cats
Jasper likes his ball
And he loses it behind the wall
He goes in the bath
And then he shakes and makes me laugh.

*Michael Todd  (10)*
*Summerfield Primary School*

## THE ESMERELDA HOTEL

The Esmerelda Hotel looks a nice sight
But if you dare to go inside
You're sure to get a terrible fright.

The Tower of Doom
Has the spookiest room
Watch out when it's a full moon.

When it's thundering and lightning
It's especially frightening
They say the attic is full of bats
And as for the cellar, it's swarming with rats.

The last time I stayed there
I thought I saw a ghost
But it was only Fred, he'd burnt the toast.

*Helen Barran  (10)*
*Summerfield Primary School*


## UNTITLED

Just a week ago
We went for a holiday in the snow
We went up mountains very high
And we very nearly reached the sky
We put our feet in some big boots
Then wrapped up warm in our ski suits.

Skiing down snowy slopes
Avoiding lots of other folks
Safely down the mountainside
Then back home to the fireside.

*Robert Durno  (8)*
*Summerfield Primary School*

## UNTITLED

Snow is cold
Snow is white
When it's been snowing
We all have
A snowball fight
When you make
A snowman it's
All good fun
But when it
Rains it begins
To run.

*Matthew Walsh (8)*
*Summerfield Primary School*

## LOVE IS INDESCRIBABLE

The way I love my caring mother,
Is different to how I'd love another.
The way my father loves my mother,
Is how I intend to love my lover.

The way I love a faithful friend,
Makes it last until the end.
The way I trust my closest friend,
Is something if broken can never mend.
*Love is indescribable.*

*Collette Allen (11)*
*Summerfield Primary School*

## WINTER

Winter is cold
Winter is grey
Winter is gloomy
Every day
Snow falls
Rain drops
Wind blows
All around
The rooftops.

*Sarah Cave  (7)*
*Summerfield Primary School*

## APOLLO THREE

There is a rocket called Apollo Three
The astronaut is called Lee
Its take-off day was May 3rd
On that day it flew like a bird
As he saw the shining sun
He was having lots of fun
Then off he flew to Mars
To see if he had any stars
But then he realised no one's there
Then he seemed not to care
So off he went to his ship
To find his favourite teddy, Pip
Then he shot off home
To see if they had built the Millennium Dome.

*Liam Shaw  (10)*
*Swinnow Primary School*

## POKÉMON

P   ikachu is a thunderbolt Pokémon
O   f all the Pokémon I like Mew
K   icking Hitmonlee is a fighting Pokémon
É   lectric Pokémon is Raichu
M   ew is the strongest Pokémon of all the Pokémon
O   nly Raichu can evolve into a crystal Pokémon
N   o Pokémon like the rain.

*Thomas Royston  (7)*
*Swinnow Primary School*


## THE SPACE STATION

The space station
Is like a scrapyard in the sky
The space station
Is a very weird creation
It fills space with an eerie cry
All the astronauts go 'Oh my'
The space station.

*Joe Fisher  (8)*
*Swinnow Primary School*


## MUSIC BOY

There once was a music boy,
He really liked S Club 7.
He soon became a singer
And had to move to Devon.

He sang a song called Broken Love,
It quickly found a place in the charts.
People queued to buy the disc,
The haunting song broke young girls' hearts.

*Andrew Heptinstall (11)*
*Swinnow Primary School*


## FEBRUARY

F   ebruary brings the wind and rain,
E   aster is coming soon,
B   right sky is sunny,
R   ound the world the sun travels,
U   p and down the sun goes,
A   round the world, nearly spring,
R   egular sky is bright,
Y   elling with excitement as February finishes.

*Jordan Hughes (8)*
*Swinnow Primary School*


## MY CUTE KITTEN

My cute kitten,
She is black with a white collar,
My cute kitten,
She is as fluffy as mittens,
She is as fresh as a dollar,
If you want kitty, just holler,
My cute kitten.

*Jessica Hodson (8)*
*Swinnow Primary School*

## THE SUNSHINE

The sun it shines,
The sun wants me to be staying.
The sun it shines,
The clouds will have been in the line.
The children are outside playing,
The sun will always be laying.
The sun it shines!

*Laura Riley  (8)*
*Swinnow Primary School*


## MYSELF

This is myself,
The stars are beautiful, like me,
This is myself,
Every day I sit on the shelf,
People always sit on my knee,
I have a boyfriend, who's a he.

*Aimee Horn  (9)*
*Swinnow Primary School*


## BLITZ

B   ombs are falling,
L   oudly,
I    t makes my ears pop
T   ime's ticking
Z   ooming fast.

*Anouska Thornton  (7)*
*Swinnow Primary School*

## WHAT'S INSIDE THE WIZARD'S POCKET?

A whining worm
A devilish dungeon
A colourful cauldron
A beetle's brain
A lolling lolly
A cackling calender
A wacking wand
A slurping slug
A mournful mountain
A whizzing whirlpool
A bucket of bubbles
A battered broomstick
A spying spellbook.

*Elizabeth Hughes  (10)*
*Swinnow Primary School*


## AN ODE TO RIDDLES

My first is in scratch but not in hill.
My second is in colours but not in bill.
My third is in hole but not in table.
My fourth is in orange but not in cable.
My fifth is in octopus but not in den.
My sixth is in lamb but not in pen.

I love to come here, I feel no hate.

What better place could educate?

What am I?

*Sarah Clifton  (10)*
*Swinnow Primary School*

## THE SUMMER FAIR

On Saturday I went to the fair,
In the corner was a dressed-up bear.
Then I saw my best friend, Marc,
He was on his way to the local park.

My friends dared me to go on the swing,
A bee came along and gave me a sting.
I fell off the swing and banged my head,
I went to the hospital and they put me in bed.

I was in hospital for a good three hours,
Before me and Mum went to Alton Towers.
Me and Mum went on all the rides,
Then back to the park to go on the slides.

Then it was time for us to go,
I tried to postpone it by walking slow.
My mum says even though the day is done,
At least we had a lot of fun!

*Jade Jones  (10)*
*Swinnow Primary School*


## TANTRUMS

I think I'll throw a tantrum
And let my temper rise,
It makes me feel great inside,
Like I'm hypnotised.

I'll be really, really mean
And throw around some books,
I'll pretend to hate everyone
And shoot them nasty looks.

Then they'll try to stop me
And beg around my knees,
I'll look at them as if they're dirt
And say, 'Get real, please.'

*Tamara Thornton (11)*
*Swinnow Primary School*


## SEASONS

Spring

Hooray springtime is here,
It comes round every year,
Sunny days are round the corner
And holidays are near.

Summer

Summertime is here at last,
It comes round really fast,
All the children play in the sun
And winter is a thing of the past.

Autumn

Autumn, leaves are turning brown,
All the people start to frown,
Knowing winter is on the way
And soon the snow starts to come down.

Winter

Slipping, sliding on the ice,
Rain and snow, not very nice,
People rushing to get home
And running round like little mice.

*Megan Roberts (10)*
*Swinnow Primary School*

## THE ROARING WIND

The roaring wind
Is wild and quick, creeping through cracks,
The roaring wind
Moves swift and silent, can't be pinned,
The wind thinks before it attacks,
I wish, I wish the wind was black,
The roaring wind.

*Megan Reilly (8)*
*Swinnow Primary School*


## SPACE DREAM

As I look up at the stars,
I wish that I could live on Mars,
I'd see rockets flying here and there,
Rockets flying everywhere,
But just for now I'll stay right here,
Dreaming about the spacestation Mir.

*Callum Dover (11)*
*Swinnow Primary School*


## BULLS, BULLS

Bulls, bulls are the best,
They are better than the rest.
I went to watch them one night
And they got into a fight.

*Mason Sidebottom (9)*
*Swinnow Primary School*

## SCOOTERS

S   coot to the hallway, shoes on very quick
C   oats if cold as well
O   ut you go to play and ride
O   utside you find your friends
T   asty things like lollies and sweets
E   ggs for dinner, then outside again
R   oads are dangerous so look before you cross
S   cooter's back in the garage, time for tea.

*Rowena Walmsley (8)*
*Swinnow Primary School*


## A RIDDLE

My first is in hat but not in bike.
My second is in ear but not in hike.
My third is in last but not in nip.
My fourth is in Leeds but not in grip.
My fifth is in on but not in hiss.
When I see my mum I say this . . .

*James Fryars (9)*
*Swinnow Primary School*


## WINDY

W   indy, cold snow
I   ce drops on the ground
N   early white all over, cold is here
D   ecember is a very cold month
Y   esterday was a very cold day.

*Ryan Longley (8)*
*Swinnow Primary School*

## THE GNOME

There once was a gnome,
Who went to Rome,
To see the Dome.
He had his tea for 50p,
He went to sleep
On a straw heap.
When he got up,
He filled his teacup.
He had his breakfast,
But it didn't last.
Then he went home,
From his journey in Rome.

*Joseph French  (10)*
*Swinnow Primary School*


## NANNY

N ice grandma
A good baby-sitter
N ever takes her eyes off me
N ow knitting a cosy jumper
Y es, my nanny is great!

*Toni Thewlis  (7)*
*Swinnow Primary School*


## SUN AND STARS

Stars are raining from the sky
But one still twinkles way up high
One sad day when it shall fall
There shall be no stars at all.

The sun and moon have said *goodbye*
Now there's no light left in the sky
As I sit here on this sad, sad day
I pray they will all come back to play.

*Alexandra Crampton  (9)*
*Swinnow Primary School*


## The Winter's Snow

Down comes the snow,
While the winds blow,
Snow, snow, snow,
Makes the traffic move slow,
Snow, snow, snow.

Snow, snow, snow,
It lays a white cloak on the ground,
Snow, snow, snow,
I'm glad to be home all safe and sound,
Snow, snow, snow.

*Gemma Hughes  (11)*
*Swinnow Primary School*


## Dolphins

Dolphins are great,
Dolphins play with me all day long,
Dolphins are great,
They really are my greatest mate,
I really like their joyful song,
I ring the dolphin bell, ding dong,
Dolphins are great.

*Jessica Teggart  (8)*
*Swinnow Primary School*

## THE MAGICAL WORLD

In the magical world of Hogwarts,
Your head will be filled with wonderful thoughts.
There's Harry with his scar,
Hermione who thinks she is a star,
In the magical world of Hogwarts.

In the magical world of Hogwarts,
Your head will be filled with wonderful thoughts.
There's Hagrid with his scruffy hair,
The Basilisks with its deadly stare,
In the magical world of Hogwarts.

In the magical world of Hogwarts,
Your head will be filled with magical thoughts.
See the squid swim a long lake,
So if I were you, I would come for your sake,
In the magical world of Hogwarts!

*Deon Thompson (10)*
*Swinnow Primary School*


## SPOOKS

A spirit glides through the gloomy night
Of your lonely attic and hall,
And who can tell what he's seeking out to find,
Howling with the racket of the whooshing wind,
It can't be a ghost you say to yourself,
Peeping over the window sill,
The garden outside is misty and still.

*Stacey Witton (9)*
*Swinnow Primary School*

## What I Found

On Monday I found a golden comb,
I put it with my precious dome.
On Tuesday I found a captain's hook,
I put it with my captain's book.
On Wednesday I found some plaited hair,
I buried it safe under the stair.
On Thursday I found a shoe made of glass,
I put it under my secret patch of grass.
On Friday I found a silver ring,
I wonder how much good luck it will bring.
On Saturday I found an earring of steel,
I put it with my wooden wheel.
On Sunday I found a piece of sail,
With all my things found, I can make an ancient tale.

*Emma Hayden  (9)*
*Swinnow Primary School*


## The Game

The moment I stepped out of the tunnel
The crowd was electrifying
I was proud to wear the white jersey
The feeling inside; the rumble in my tummy!

The crowd roared and the whistle blew
Then the ball came to me
I had a shot . . .
It was swirling and hurling like a rocket
It went in the corner of the net
*Goooal!*

*Andrew Doogan  (10)*
*Swinnow Primary School*

## WHAT'S INSIDE A WIZARD'S POCKET

A singing sword
A dancing donkey
A wonky wizard
A wiggly white worm
A magical mat
A nutty nut
A worrying wart
A slurping slug.

*Luke Hird  (10)*
*Swinnow Primary School*


## THE BLACK SPIDER

The black spider,
She is frightening and creaky,
The black spider,
She scares every passing rider,
She is large and very freaky,
The spider is really cheeky,
The black spider.

*Faye Mills  (9)*
*Swinnow Primary School*


## MY HOLIDAY

I can't wait to go on holiday,
With my mum and dad.
I love living in Leeds
But the weather is really bad!

I can't wait to go on holiday,
Can't wait for the plane to land.
I'll run straight down to the beach
And play in the sea and sand.

*Samantha Farr  (10)*
*Swinnow Primary School*


## MY SCHOOL TEACHER

My school teacher
She looks like a big sticky bun
My school teacher
She yells like a screaming preacher
She can brighten up like the sun
She teaches maths to make it fun
My school teacher.

*Craig Bell  (9)*
*Swinnow Primary School*


## DECEMBER

D   ecember brings snow,
E   arly snow on grass,
C   hristmas celebrated everywhere,
E   very year Santa comes,
M   erry Christmas to everyone
B   ulb on the Christmas tree
E   vening, Christmas dinner,
R   ound the world Santa travels.

*Luke Whitehouse  (7)*
*Swinnow Primary School*

## TWIRLING LEAVES

Leaves twirl off trees,
rumble upon the ground and crackle.
Early evening, dark evening creeps
leaves stay silent.
After twirling leaves blow upon
the ground and rustle.
Valleys begin to mist, walk through it
you will see leaves twirling.
Ears cold, leaves begin to die
and scrunch and crackle.
Spinning leaves fade away and the
colours begin to go brown.

*Matthew Stead  (10)*
*Swinnow Primary School*


## THE GOLDEN SPOON

There was a young boy on the moon
Who lost his golden spoon
As the days went by
He started to cry
He does hope he'll find it soon

There was a young boy on the moon
Who found his golden spoon
As the days went by
He made a mince pie
He hopes he can eat with his spoon soon.

*Helen Lambert  (9)*
*Swinnow Primary School*

## EMERGENCY

Red alert
Red alert
I've dropped my lolly in the dirt
SOS
SOS
I've got custard down my dress
999
999
I rode my bike through the washing line
Ambulance, ambulance
And make it quick, I think I'm going to be sick.

*Laura Atkins  (10)*
*Swinnow Primary School*


## BLEAK MIDWINTER

B   lood-red berries iced with snow,
L   ively lights illuminate the streets,
E   veryone sits happily around the fire singing merrily
A   mazing snowflakes drifting down outside
K   een, cold night air

M   idnight strikes onto twelve,
I   n the morning the entire world will be transformed
D   rifts of snow fill the night sky
W   arm, watery sun is rising once more
I   cicles melt in the wintry beam of sunlight
N   othing stirring not even a mouse
T   rees silhouetted against the sky
E   veryone awakes to a cold winter morning
R   ushing out in the first winter snow!

*Jennifer Best  (11)*
*The Froebelian School*

## WINTER

B   lack is the night,
L   anes covered in snow,
E   very tree branch, frozen,
A   nd still,
K   iller cold freezes my toes.

M   y gloves are sodden with the melting snow
I   nside people are warm,
D   elighted to be gathered around the fire,
W   aiting for the Christmas dinner.
I   n the deep, black, velvet sky,
N   ight stars are bravely shining,
T   winkling high up in the sky.
E   arly morning is now dawning,
R   ays of pale pink sun tint the newly-laid snow.

*Jake Thornton  (10)*
*The Froebelian School*


## FIREWORKS

Catherine wheel sparkling all around,
turning into wonderful colours,
red, blue, yellow and then fading away.

Rockets firing off in all directions
is what you can hear in the dark, dark moonlight.

Traffic lights turning into red, orange, green,
waiting for the cars to go,
shooting their colours through the night.

Roman candles firing white spray into the dark, cold night.

Bangers making loud noises in the dark night air,
screeching and wailing!

Silver blast, echoes from the past,
so remember, remember the fifth of November.

*Jamie Flounders  (10)*
*The Froebelian School*


## BRIGHT STARRY NIGHT

B   rilliant, beaming, blazing lights
R   evealing, showing the shimmering stars
I   n the cold, black night
G   olden with the daylight of a wish
H   iding during daytime behind the sun so bright
T   imid and frightened of the light.

S   tars so bright in the dark misty night
T   o brighten the run-up to Christmas
A   ll because of a mystery of a baby boy
R   eady to discover more about him
R   eady with a Christingle
Y   et nothing is gained until his birth.

N   obody was not wishing
I   n their beds, all dreaming
G   uided to an unknown place
H   appy to wake up in the morning
T   o open surprises and mysterious parcels.

*Emma Bolton  (10)*
*The Froebelian School*

## BRIGHT STARRY NIGHT

B  right stars emerge out of the night sky,
R  eflecting on the frozen lake.
I  mages are silver in the moonlight,
G  rowing shadows come to life, swaying in the icy breeze.
H  ootings of owls echo in the dark valleys,
T  he frosted grass shimmers like crystal dust.

S  now slowly settles on the cold, hard ground,
T  all trees tower above their long, dark shadows.
A  nd all around the Earth is freezing,
R  iver waters forever flowing,
R  esisting of the cold night air,
Y  earning, restless, foaming and surging.

N  octurnal animals scuttle about frantically, hungry for food,
I  magining warmer days of plenty.
G  listening eyes of the cunning fox,
H  unting for its unsuspecting prey,
T  ill morning dawns beckoning a new day.

*Bethan Layfield  (11)*
*The Froebelian School*

## BLEAK MIDWINTER

B  lack, the night, nobody stirs
L  ight's fading into darkness
E  verthing's frozen except for me and a ginger cat purring on a wall
A  ll alone, shut out from the warmth
K  iller winds howling all around, whisking anything light off
                                                        the ground

M  aybe the frosty, wintry nightmare will never end
I  cy frost covers the ground like a white carpet
D  ropping like stones, hail falls out of the sky
W  inter, the evil season of bitter cold
I  ce settles on the pavement, ready to make anyone slip
N  asty, ghastly winds die and leave a vicious breeze behind
T  he night begins to fade into the distance
E  verything starts to wake
R  eady for the day ahead.

*Emma Hutson  (11)*
*The Froebelian School*


## REMEMBER, REMEMBER THE FIFTH OF NOVEMBER

Catherine wheels whizzing, wheeling, speeding up,
spraying golden dust.
Soaring high, shooting up, fizzing, dancing fireworks.
Rockets zooming up with bursting sparks flashing in the air.
Soaring high, shooting up, fizzing, dancing fireworks.
Shooting stars wailing and soaring high into the firelit sky.
Soaring high, shooting up, fizzing, dancing fireworks.
Bangers flare, dazzling with a myriad of pops and bangs.
Soaring high, shooting up, fizzing, dancing fireworks.
Sparklers spluttering and hissing, glowing in the coal black sky.
Soaring high, shooting up, fizzing, dancing fireworks.

*Lucy Hicks  (10)*
*The Froebelian School*

## BLEAK MIDWINTER

B leak is the sky, nothing is
L iving, nothing is moving,
E verything is dead.
A ll people asleep in their beds.
K nives of ice hang from rooftops.

M idnight strikes mournfully
I n the pitch-black
D ark, cold, bleak mid
W inter night.
I nvisible ghouls, floating in the night
N ight, everyone slumbers on
T ime ticking away
E nding the frozen nocturn
R eady for another day.

*James Saville (11)*
*The Froebelian School*


## FIREWORKS

Catherine wheels spinning in the night sky,
Come and see the amber and golden sparks fly!

Traffic lights smoking in the garden with
Colours sparkling in green and red and gold,
Sending ghostly shadows into the trees.

Rockets screaming into the night sky and
Bursting into a multitude of colours,
Before sending sparkling raindrops showering down
To the earth.

Colours burst out from the smouldering volcano,
Spluttering spurting out the last silver
Sparks and dies.

Sparklers like wands in the hands of excited
Children twinkle and splutter as they spell out
Magical words in the night sky.

*Anya Zia  (10)*
*The Froebelian School*


## BRIGHT STARRY NIGHT

B   lazing light of a Christmas fire,
R   oaring, crackling, with its dancing light,
I    n the snow-covered streets
G   angs of children play in the moonlight,
H   igh above them, bright stars shine in the night sky
T   winkling like newly-cut diamonds.

S   adly night will soon unfold,
T   urning into day,
A   nd all the stars will ebb and fade away to
R   ise again once more,
R   ound the seasons, round the days,
Y   ears go by but the stars live on.

N   aked branches reaching skyward,
I    cicles sparkle and glitter,
G   olden leaves long fallen,
H   oly night, Christmas night, commemorates
T   he birth of Jesus.

*Cameron Johnston  (10)*
*The Froebelian School*

## BRIGHT STARRY NIGHT

B   lack is the night
R   unning through the
I   ce-cold snow
G   athering coat about me
H   oping for warmth
T   errified of slipping on the icy streets

S   heets of danger, shadows
T   easing me all
A   round.
R   acing images, monsters lurking
R   ound each corner
Y   et there is nothing

N   othing to frighten me but my
I   magination, going mad
G   one is the fear as I gaze around in bright moonshine
H   igh in the sky stars are alive
T   winkling pinpricks in the dead of night banishing the fear of night.

*Hannah Brown (11)*
*The Froebelian School*

## BRIGHT STARRY NIGHT

B  lowing blistering wind rustling in the trees,
R  oaring, wrapping itself round cold bodies,
I  cing over the wet grass,
G  iving numb fingers and numb toes,
H  eat fading away gradually,
T  rickling snow drifting down to Earth.

S  tars scattered over the black sky,
T  rees reaching into space,
A  ll is eerily, spooky and silent,
R  ocketing stars flying through the sky,
R  eeling the silver frost over the ground,
Y  earning for an ounce of warmth.

N  obody else will brave this bleak midwinter night,
I  t's so cold and deeply dark
G  radually snow drifts into nooks and crannies
H  urrying home into warmth and welcome
T  eeth are chattering but you know that journey's end's in sight.

*Lewis Lamb  (10)*
*The Froebelian School*

## BLEAK MIDWINTER NIGHT

B  lack, dark night
L  ittle luminous rays of light brighten up the sky,
E  mpty streets - everyone safe inside,
A  nd drinking hot cocoa in front of the fire,
K  iddies are excited watching the snow fluttering in the cold breeze.

M  en struggling Christmas trees home,
I  n the crowded darkening street.
D  eep snow falls all around us,
W  onderful, marvellous festival time.
I  n the cold, clear, starry night,
N  icholas rides through the deep velvet sky.
T  ired children struggle to keep awake,
E  mpty stockings wait to be filled,
R  udolph paws impatiently on the roof.

N  oiseless snow falls gently all around,
I  cicles hang from every branch and twig.
G  ifts are piled up underneath the tree,
H  appy children laugh and cheer
T  o see the gifts that they have received.

*Amy Chapman  (10)*
*The Froebelian School*

## BLEAK MIDWINTER

B itter wind, whistling and wailing through the trees,
L ights flickering in the windows,
E erie shadows creep across the dewy ground,
A long the floors of the forest,
K eeping a silent guard.

M idnight strikes, all is quiet,
I ndigo skies where the stars shine through,
D reaming of the new day dawning as
W inter's watery moon fades away,
I n the sky the snowflakes dance and swirl,
N ew-laid blankets cover every garden path,
T rees are adorned with a touch of frost,
E choed tones of the distant church bells,
R eminds the world of Christmas Day.

*Harriet Carter  (11)*
*The Froebelian School*


## FIREWORKS

Catherine wheels spin round fast in many magical colours.
Crackling, snapping, whirling all around.
Roman candles soar into the clouds spurting out golden colours.
Crackling, snapping, whirling all around.
Marigolds shoot at a great height exploding, glowing gold.
Crackling, snapping, whirling all around.
Rockets are loud when they *bang* in the sky.
Crackling, snapping, whirling all around.
Bangers stay on the ground going *boom, boom*,
Uncolourful but deafening.

*Jessica Smith  (11)*
*The Froebelian School*

## BONFIRE POEM

Jumping jacks hop and leap up high,
furiously spinning round and vanishing,
different colours catch the eye and
then is left to slowly, slowly die.

Spinning, flying, zooming and slowly dying.

A fountain is lit and begins to spurt out small rockets
of blue, red, gold and silver
and the sparks begin to fade and slowly it concludes.

Spinning, flying, zooming and slowly dying.

The rocket is lit and we all stand still
as it zooms up into the sky casting masses of golden light.

Spinning, flying, zooming and slowly dying.

The banger is lit and the finale is here,
everybody holds their ears and the first bang jumps up high
and explodes, creating a huge echo around the valley,
*bang, bang, bang, bang, bang.*

Spinning, flying, zooming and slowly dying.

*Edward Cottle  (10)*
*The Froebelian School*

## BRIGHT STARRY NIGHT

B   eautiful stars shining, glistening in the sky.
R   elaxing inside, keeping warm from the cold.
I    cicles hang from the trees.
G   alaxies of stars lighting up the sky.
H   ampers of snow pile up on the street.
T   opping trees in layers of snow.

S   ilence outside, frozen windows.
T   oo glad I am to be inside.
A   frozen landscape through the frost of the window.
R   ioting snow blowing in swirls with the wind.
R   uby stars shining in the sky.
Y   ellow lamps brighten up the night.

N   ight is covered with a blanket of snow.
I    ced over with a silver frost.
G   listening icicles all around.
H   anging in suspense like animated drips.
T   rickling like hardened wax from snuffed-out candles.

*Daniel Morley  (10)*
*The Froebelian School*


## THE BEE THAT CHASES ME

It hangs around my garden shed,
When I'm around there, it's on my head,
It chases me all the time,
*Ahhhh!* It's after me,
Is it the sun
That makes the bee come and chase me?

*Joseph Geldart  (11)*
*Tranmere Park CP School*

## MY BROTHER

M  y brother's name is William
Y  ou would love him if you knew him

B  ig brown eyes
R  osy red cheeks
O  n the football pitch every Sunday
T  ackling like a demon
H  e always wins the ball
E  ach and every game
R  emember, he is my brother!

*Sam Wormald (11)*
*Tranmere Park CP School*

## MY BEST FRIEND
*(Richard Truswell)*

My best friend is witty and fast
In a race he never comes last.
At a race when I'm ahead by a mile
He'll just zoom past and flash a cocky smile.
My best friend is quite a sporty guy,
When he's running you think he's going to fly,
Also in football he is quite good to defend his end
Because he's my best friend.

*Liam Matthews (10)*
*Tranmere Park CP School*

# A-Z ON GIRLS

Always chatting
Bestest friends forever
Caring
Devious and daring
Exciting and eligible
Forever I'll be your friend
Glamorous
Helpful
Independent
Jokey and jolly
Kind
Loving
Mature
Never nasty
Often endlessly talking about the boy they fancy
Perfect chum
Queer
Receptive
Sharing
They are always there for you when you need them
Understanding
Very big phone bill
Worrying about what they look like
Xtra special
Yapping all day long
Zzzzzzz very tired after a sleep-over.

*Catriona Campbell (11)*
*Tranmere Park CP School*

## THE FOUR SEASONS

Spring

Spring, a time to enjoy the sun, green grass and no rain,
The sun is out longer, more time to play!
Birds cheep on sunny days,
People sneeze, as hayfever comes to ruin some people's days.

Summer

Summer, the leaves on the trees recover from winter,
Children go so playful you cannot stop them from going outside
and playing,
To calm the children down, an ice cream man comes to town,
Children lick their lips as the ice cream melts onto the floor.

Autumn

Autumn, the leaves on trees go orange, yellow, brown and red as
they drop off trees,
Making a pile on the floor,
The nights get darker,
The day turns into night at five o'clock.

Winter

Winter, snow falls on my nose,
The frost froze the hose,
The trees are now bare as animals hibernate,
The night gets darker, earlier.

*Joshua Stayman  (11)*
*Tranmere Park CP School*

## MY SHELL

Soft, pink and small,
A perfect oval,
Rippled like a calm sea,
Soft like a baby's skin.
Insignificant and tiny against a big dark world,
That looms over it, large and forbidding.
It has seen many people and places and has lived to tell.
Inside my shell I am a welcome guest.
The sea is a faraway soothing sound,
Rushing and falling, rushing and falling.
To be inside my shell is like nothing before anything.
Everything is bathed in a rose pink glow that glimmers and dims.
Forever searching. So soft and lulling, a sleepy tide washes over me,
Rushing and falling, rushing and falling like the sea.
Though hard to fight, sleep is easy . . .
I wake up. It is night, I am still in my shell, stuck in a big empty
                                                    black hole forever.
The waves of life are an endless sea, tossing and turning.
The sea is my home, my life, my future, my past, my beginning
                                                    and my end.

Waves come and go but a shell stays forever.
Forever looking for that one dream,
That dream to become big, that dream to become small,
That dream that has been with you for all eternity.
That one wish, that one hope, that one fantasy.
That one shining bit of fame and glory.
And now it's gone. I'll miss the way it stayed in my pocket when
                                                    everything else fell out.
Without my shell I won't be able to listen to the waves lapping at
                                                    the shore.

Soft, pink and small,
A perfect oval,
Rippled like a calm sea.

*Becky Goult  (10)*
*Tranmere Park CP School*

## THE DOUGHNUT

This doughnut is big,
This doughnut is round,
This doughnut that I have found.

This is no ordinary doughnut,
It's covered in icing,
It's also very enticing.

This doughnut has sprinkles,
This doughnut has cream,
But I really want to scream.

The thing annoying me in my head,
Is this doughnut's from under my *bed!*

*Matthew Alderson (11)*
*Tranmere Park CP School*


## SPACE

Space is a lonely
Place to be, so come and sit
On a star with me

When you are up here
You'll see how lonely space is
Why not go back home

He has gone home
Now I'm up here alone
On this star of mine.

*Conor Dawson (10)*
*Tranmere Park CP School*

# THE SUMMER HOLIDAYS

I explode out of school on the last day of term,
It's all fun from now on and nothing to learn.
My time is my own for six weeks of fun,
The endless days of freedom have only just begun.

My bedtime has changed from early to late,
But I'm still getting up at quarter to eight.
I play out on the street from morning to night,
Without a bicker or even a fight.

Football, rugby, biking is my best,
In football I shout, ''Ere on me chest!'
The holiday has finally come to an end,
School is once again lurking round the bend!

*Sam Prus  (10)*
*Tranmere Park CP School*


# MY BEST FRIEND
*(Liam Matthews)*

My best friend is very funny, he can dance around like a bunny.
My best friend is a friend to trust, my best friend eats his crusts.
My best friend can play a game of golf, my best friend does an
impression of Rolf.
My best friend never starts fights and he's not a girl so he
doesn't wear tights.
My best friend is very clever and he walks to school
whatever the weather.
My best friend likes lots of gore, but he wouldn't break anyone's jaw.
My best friend, my best friend, our friendship will never end.

*Richard Truswell  (11)*
*Tranmere Park CP School*

## POEM

A poem about an animal
What shall I choose?
I know, I thought a kangaroo!
It bounces and hops and never stops,
No, that won't get my poem in this book,
They probably won't even take a look.

A poem about time, now I'm really stuck,
But wait, what about a clock?
It ticks and tocks and never stops,
No, that won't get my poem read,
This poetry's not getting to my head.

A poem about anything,
What am I to do?
Let me think, what about you!
You think and look at poems from this book.
Are you reading this?
What do you think?
Is it enjoyable or is it just ink?
I don't care, I've come to the end,
*Thank goodness!*
This poetry is driving me round the bend!

*Katie Kelly  (10)*
*Tranmere Park CP School*


## THE CAT ACROSS THE ROAD

The cat across the road caterwauls all night,
He starts at 8pm and ends at 1am,
I wish I could pick him up and strangle him.

The cat across the road caterwauls all night,
I'm tired, I've even tried sleeping pills,
But still the cat sings on.

The cat across the road caterwauls all night,
I suppose I'll have to get used to it,
I now don't mind at all.

The cat across the road caterwauls no more,
It feels quite strange without him,
I can get to sleep, but I don't want to,
It's very strange, I want the caterwauling cat back!

*Kate Donnelly (10)*
*Tranmere Park CP School*


## PLANETS

The heavenly bodies of the sky are Mercury, Venus,
Earth, Mars, Jupiter, Saturn, Uranus, Neptune, Pluto and the sun.

The night is like a blanket where stars and planets peep through.

Mercury plays hide and seek as it stays close by the sun.

Venus twinkles in the twilight sky.

One day I will leave the Earth and fly to the moon
and look down at my home so far away.

Calling Mars, calling Mars, is anyone there?

Jupiter, the biggest planet of them all.

Uranus, Neptune and Pluto are very far away.
Only Voyager 2 has ever been that far.

The sun, the centre of our universe on which we all depend.
How dark and miserable our world would be without
its light and warmth.

When you look out at the starry sky think of those planets zooming by.

*Jonathan Holt (10)*
*Tranmere Park CP School*

# I'M ON A VOYAGE

I'm on a voyage
To see the moon
To reach the sun
And travel through space.

I'm on a voyage
To rescue treasure
To find stolen jewels
And uncover mysteries.

I'm on a voyage
To enter a world
To ride dragons
And learn magic tricks.

I'm on a voyage
To stop all evil
To save the world
And make peace on Earth.

I'm on a voyage
To read plenty of books
To climb into heads
And engross in the thoughts of others.

I'm on a voyage
To climb Mount Everest
To walk across the Sahara
And swim the English Channel.

I'm on a voyage
To always have fun
To laugh with others
And enjoy life.

Life would be perfect in every way
If we all try harder every day.

*Jessica Macdonald (11)*
*Tranmere Park CP School*


## ANIMALS

Animals have four legs,
Animals have a head,
Animals have fur or flat skin,
Some eat out of a bin.

Animals live everywhere,
Even in houses,
Animals can be good
And some live in the wood.

Animals are scary,
But some are like a fairy,
Some animals are cute
And some even live on fruit.

Animals can be tall,
Or some can be small,
Some can be fat,
Or some can be the size of a mat.

*Matthew Bowles (11)*
*Tranmere Park CP School*

## CHOCOLATE

Chocolate is nice,
Chocolate is yummy,
Chocolate lives inside my tummy.

I can't help myself, that dark brown creamy chocolate,
When you put it in your mouth it feels as smooth as silk.

Chocolate is nice,
Chocolate is yummy,
Chocolate lives inside my tummy.

It sits there on the shelf saying *'Eat Me, Eat Me'*
I can't help myself, my hand goes in, all of a sudden the
Chocolate is *gone!*

Chocolate is nice,
Chocolate is yummy,
Chocolate lives inside my tummy.

*Matthew Nolson  (11)*
*Tranmere Park CP School*


## MY FRIEND, SAM

M  y friend Sam is kind and thoughtful
Y  ou stop and say, 'How do you do?'

F  riday is his best day
R  unning is his game
I  n the week he has some fun
E  ven when he fell in the mud
N  ever cries just smiles
D  ances at discos like mad.

*James Davey  (10)*
*Tranmere Park CP School*

## TEACHERS

Some teachers are kind, some are horrid,
Some are just plain boring,
The boring type drone on and on
Until everyone starts snoring.

Some teachers are kind, some are boring,
Some are totally horrid,
They shout and shout and shout some more
Until their throats get very sore.

Some teachers are boring, some are horrid,
Some are really kind,
They're very patient and understanding
And most things they don't mind.

The teacher we have at the moment
Is as kind as they can get
He helps us when we need him
He is the best yet!

*Emily Alderson  (11)*
*Tranmere Park CP School*


## ANIMALS

Some are furry, some are bald,
Some will not keep quite at all.

Some live in water, some live on land,
Some live in the hot warm sand.

Some live in their warm, small cages
And some live in pet shops for ages and ages.

*Alexandra Wright  (11)*
*Tranmere Park CP School*

## THE TELEVISION

I'm the television,
Living in the sitting room.
Never moving,
With five channels on On Digital.

I can still remember the day I was bought.
Two adults walked into the shop,
The man asked 'We need a widescreen, can you do the job?'
'Certainly' the assistant replied and the next thing I knew I was in a
box.

That was twenty years ago, they've got two children now.
Nowadays I'm hardly used,
Because the children go to school
And a while later, the adults go to work.

My favourite channels are comedies,
Blackadder and Harry Enfield are best.
By far the worst are pre-school shows,
I hate Play Days and The Magic Roundabout.

It's a nice life being a TV,
I'm never in a hurry.
I'm a lifeline for my owners
Saving them from boredom.

*Emma Davies  (11)*
*Tranmere Park CP School*

## WAR AND PEACE

W oeful men collapsing
A mbushed troops afraid
R ecruits firing helplessly
F rightful sights seen
A nguished soldiers dying
R ampant death rejoicing
E veryone fearfully sobbing

H appy friends chatting
A ll Christians rejoice
R aucous crowds cheering
M erry children playing
O verjoyed youngsters dancing
N ational celebrations commence
Y esterday forgotten.

*Iona Boyle  (11)*
*Weetwood Primary School*

## THE MISTAKE

I was walking up the pathway,
I knew what was going to happen,
I was shaking like a leaf,
I was as cold as an ice cube.
I felt like I had butterflies in my tummy,
Nearer and nearer I came to the gate
And . . . the playground was empty,
There was no one to be seen!
It was like in space, you could even hear a pin drop.

*Harriet Munday  (10)*
*Weetwood Primary School*

# THE WRITER OF THIS POEM

The writer of this poem is
Cooler than a fridge
As sly as a fox
As strong as you can get

As clever as a computer
As fit as a fiddle
As quick as a mouse
As skilful as a cheetah

As brave as a lion
As agile as a cat
As fast as the speed of light
Is brilliant at sport
Is as hard as nails

The writer of this poem
Is perfect, if you please
He excels in everything he does
This guy's the bee's knees!
But if you really knew him
He's just a real tease.

*Arthur Brown  (10)*
*Weetwood Primary School*


# ANGELS

Angels are wondrous things,
They dance and prance and play and sing,
Golden halos and wings pearly white,
They shine in the shimmering light.

*Maude Churchill  (11)*
*Weetwood Primary School*

## HORSE KENNING

Daylight-dancer
  Moonlight-prancer
   Hay-eater
    Silent-sleeper
     Wind-wild
      Riding-child
       Track-racer
       Fast-pacer
      Tail-flicker
     People-kicker
    Grass-muncher
   Apple-cruncher
  Strong-trotter
 Mane-tosser
Faithful-friend
Till the end.

*Subpreet Deu & Alice Fellowes  (10)*
*Weetwood Primary School*


## DOG KENNING

Bone-cruncher
Mutton-muncher
Tail-wagger
Bone-bagger
Car-barker
Friendly-larker
Cat-chaser
Super-racer
Food-guzzler
Friend-nuzzler.

*Alexander Henderson & Patrick Grier  (11)*
*Weetwood Primary School*

## THE WRITER OF THIS POEM

The writer of this poem is as
cute as a puppy,
happy as a lamb,
lovely as a summer scene,
fluffy as a lamb.
The writer of this poem has
hair as nice as chocolate,
complexion smooth as cream
tastes as good as kind and peace,
a smile like a sunlight beam.
The writer of this poem is as
amazing as a miracle,
as cool as cool could be.
The writer of this poem is . . .
Me! Me! Me!

*Jenny McGowan  (10)*
*Weetwood Primary School*


## LION KENNING

Fierce-chaser
Silent-pacer
Claw-scratcher
Fast-catcher
Teeth-tearing
Surprisingly-daring
Paw-pouncer
Jumping-bouncer
Meat-eater
Animal-beater
Evil-spyer
Heart of fire.

*Harry Clifford & Robert May  (10)*
*Weetwood Primary School*

## RABBIT KENNING

Carrot
Crunchers
Grass
Muncher
Burrow
Digger
Ears
Bigger
Tail
Itcher
Whisker
Twitcher
Leg
Thumper

Wrong
Nothing
Long
Teeth
Stuffer
Vegetable
Fluffer
Fur
Chopper
Lettuce
Hopper
Land
Jumper
High

*Michael Russam  (10)*
*Weetwood Primary School*


## THE NEIGHBOUR

There is a lady down our street,
Who we hardly ever get to meet.
She very rarely comes outside
But if she does, I tend to hide.
She shoos kids away like dogs or cats,
It wouldn't surprise me if she kept pet bats.
Maybe she's friendly, I don't really know,
Perhaps I should go and say hello
But what would happen? What would she do?
She might take me or maybe *you!*
She might make me sneeze or make me itch
(But I'll tell you something, I think she's a witch!)

*Jenny Roy  (10)*
*Weetwood Primary School*

# A MONSTER UNDER THE BED

He's never there when the lights are on,
Or when Mum and Dad are near
Only when the lights go out,
That's when he appears.

There's a monster under the bed,
With long thin arms and short fat legs,
Twisted toes and knobbly knees
He loves to eat mouldy peas.

So the moral of the story is
Never ever get out of bed!

*Emma Rodriguez-Saona  (10)*
*Weetword Pimary School*


# THE WRITER OF THIS POEM

The writer of this poem is
as cool as an ice cube
as sticky as gel
as scientific as a testing tube
as strong as a house
as smooth as chocolate
as nippy as a mouse
as oval as a rugby ball
as fast as the wind
I know I am not tall
But I'm afraid that's all
(Or so the poet says.)

*Robert May  (10)*
*Weetwood Primary School*

# THE WRITER OF THIS POEM

The writer of this poem
Is as bright as a newborn chick
Her golden locks flow
As slow
As a ripple on a stream
She's as gentle as a breeze
As strong as a hard *metal* brick

The writer of this poem
Is as plain as you can see
The marvel in the class
And as cool as cool can be

So if you see this girl walking down the street
Just remember this
Beware
She might jump out at you and scare
You like a hare

*Elinor Briggs  (11)*
*Weetwood Primary School*


# WAR AND PEACE

War
Fighting, terror,
Cruel laughter, screaming, pain,
Gunfire, crying, smiling, birdsong,
Carefree mirth, singing, joy,
Affection, happiness,
Peace.

*Isabel Nelson  (10)*
*Weetwood Primary School*

## THE WRITER OF THIS POEM

The writer of this poem
Is as small as a mouse
As quick as light
As clean as a dolphin

As tough as a rock
As sharp as a blade
As strong as a lion
As fiddly as a fib

As smooth as fur
As quick as a track
As beautiful as a rose
As clever as a cat

The writer of this poem is
Me!

*Danielle Dovey  (11)*
*Weetwood Primary School*


## THE WRITER OF THIS POEM

The writer of this poem
Is as sly as a spy
As clever as Einstein
Stronger than the sea

More skilful than a footballer
Faster than a Ferrari
Cooler than a freezer
As busy as a bee

Taller than a building
As stable as a chair
More fearsome than a hunter
And goes everywhere

The writer of this poem
Can jump higher than the stars
He says he's been to Mars.

*Alexander Henderson  (11)*
*Weetwood Primary School*


## WEREWOLF

Teeth-gnashing
Throat-gashing
Meat-eating
Food-seeking
Loud-roaring
Fierce-clawing
House-trashing
Window-smashing
Child-slicing
Flesh-dicing
Moon-howling
Night-prowling
Lamb-munching
Bone-crunching
Hair-scruffy
Big-toughie.

*John Nicholson & Joe Julier  (11)*
*Weetwood Primary School*

# Fox

Moon-howler
Night-prowler
Claw-fighter
Furious-biter
Bin-sniffer
Cat-biffer
Rubbish-snatcher
Tree-scratcher
Sly-stealer
Cunning-dealer
Midnight-stalker
Sleek-walker
Vicious-clawer
Sharp-gnawer
Rabbit-eater
Fierce-beater
Day-sleeper
Dark-creeper.

*Anna Furniss & Ciara O'Brien  (10)*
*Weetwood Primary School*


# The Writer Of This Poem

The writer of this poem
Is cooler than an ice cube
As slick as oil
And can fly like an eagle

As fast as the speed of light
As clever as a calculator
As hard as nails
And is brave enough to do anything which isn't nasty

As good as gold
As calm as a leopard
As full of fun (maybe)
But is never bored (until it's boring)

The writer of this poem
Is learning every day
He sits on a golden throne
Because he is the king
It's just a joke, OK.

*George Adams  (10)*
*Weetwood Primary School*


## THE WRITER OF THIS POEM

The writer of this poem
Is as cool as can be,
As silky as cat's fur,
And as lovely as a mega star,

As fast as the wind,
As skilful as an eagle,
As sweet as candy
And as cute as cuddly toys.

The writer of this poem
Is as amazing as can be!

The writer of this poem
Is cool, cool, cool!
Brill! Brill! Brill!

The writer of this poem
Is . . . Me!

*Briony Fisher  (10)*
*Weetwood Primary School*

# THE WRITER OF THIS POEM

The writer of this poem
Is taller than Big Ben,
As cool as an ice box,
Stronger than a million men,

As smart as a computer,
As fit as a fiddle,
As handsome as a pop star,
As tricky as a riddle,

As bright as a light bulb
As fast as a hare,
As slick as hair gel,
As rich as a millionaire,

As tough as a tiger,
As cute as a cuddly bear,
As spotless as a spring clean,
As smooth as a baby's hair,

As proud as a shark
In the ocean free.
This couldn't just be anyone,
Anyone but me!

*Andrew Palliser (10)*
*Weetwood Primary School*


# THE WRITER OF THIS POEM

The writer of this poem
Is bigger than a gate
As pale as cream
As small as a bee

As strong as metal
As fast as wind
As brown-haired as mud
As kind as a butterfly
As clean as paint
As good as gold
The writer of this poem is not me.

*Hannah Woods  (10)*
*Weetwood Primary School*


## THE WRITER OF THIS POEM

The writer of this poem
Is as soft as a teddy bear
As flowing as a river
As stable as a chair

As dainty as a ballerina
As quiet as a mouse
As clever as a parrot
As tall as a house

As giddy as a school girl
As careful as a cat
As clean as a Hoover
As furry as a mat

But if you really met this girl
You certainly wouldn't agree -
The things I've said are not quite true
Just look for yourself and see.

*Jenny Roy  (10)*
*Weetwood Primary School*